Quotes on Sex, Love & Marriage

Quotes on Sex, Love & Marriage

Quotes on Sex, Love & Marriage

ISBN # 978-0-615-73320-3

Original Compilation Copyright © March 25, 1988

TXu 319-449

Re-copyright update November 2012 by original Editor:

Txu 1-839-337

Robert H Williams
P.O. Box 392
Plattsburgh N.Y. 12901
rhw007@twcny.rr.com
http://MyCommonSensePolitics
Http://commonsensecentral.net

Quotes on Sex, Love & Marriage

Chapters

Quotes on Sex & Sexual Attraction -------- pg 5

Quotes on Love & Romance -------- pg 75

Quotes on Marriage & Weddings -------- pg 120

Quotes on Women -------- pg 155

Quotes on Men -------- pg 187

Quotes on Women & Men -------- pg 206

Quotes on Family and Everything Else -------- pg 240

Quotes on Sex, Love & Marriage

Quotes on Sex & Sexual Attraction

Before you can score you must first have a goal. Greek Proverb

An apple pie without some cheese is like a kiss without a squeeze. English Rhyme

An apple pie without some whipped cream is like a kiss without emotion. Pema

An apple pie without some ice cream is like a kiss without passion. Bobby

Girls who don't repulse men's advances advance men's pulses. Playboy

It is remarkable how many impure things a prude can discover that nobody else can discover. Unknown

Whether or not a girl can be had for a song depends on a man's pitch. Playboy

Making love to a woman too many times is like scratching a place that doesn't itch anymore. Playboy

Loving a woman never satisfies her; you've got to make love to her. Unknown

Quotes on Sex, Love & Marriage

Sex is only dirty if it's done right. American Proverb

There are no premature babies, only delayed weddings.
American Proverb

Absence and a friendly neighbor washeth away love. English Proverb

A chorus girl is like a zoo: she comes in like a lamb, meets a wolf, gets sly as a fox, and winds up with a mink. Unknown

Small boy to slightly smaller girl: "Are you the opposite sex, or am I?" Unknown

How do you tell girl pancakes from boy pancakes? By the way they're stacked. Unknown

The wives of a progressive Indian reserve have taken to swapping husbands. They call it passing the buck. Unknown

Two very small boys were playing marbles together when a very, very pretty little girl walked by. One of the boys exclaimed fervently to his pal, "Brother, when I stop hating girls, she's the one I'm going to stop hating first!" Unknown

A topless waitress is a girl you look up to, very, very slowly.
Unknown

One is never too old to yearn. Italian Proverb

Quotes on Sex, Love & Marriage

She who is silent consents. French Proverb

You know, humanly speaking, there is a certain degree of temptation which will overcome any virtue. Samuel Johnson

A clever, ugly man every now and then is successful with the ladies, but a handsome fool is irresistible. William M. Thackeray

He is a fool that kisseth the maid when he may kiss the mistress. English Proverb

I've been on a calendar, but never on time. Marilyn Monroe

A secretary is a clever girl who can add, or a cute girl who can distract. Unknown

Pornography is any writing, picture, or form of entertainment that is too sexplicit. Unknown

Sex is an emotion in motion. Mae West

When a woman is openly bad she is then at her best. Latin Proverb

The girl who blushes needs no makeup. Russian Proverb

Gravity is a law that's defied by three things: taxes, prices, and bikinis. Unknown

Quotes on Sex, Love & Marriage

Hindsight is what a woman needs most when buying shorts. Unknown

Interest is what a woman without principle draws. Unknown

A lover is a sweetheart, not a sweet tart. Unknown

The function of muscle is to pull and not to push, except in the case of the genitals and the tongue. Leonardo da Vinci

Lips, however rosy, must be fed. Scottish Proverb

A mistress is a woman who is known by the company that keeps her. Unknown

Orgasm is the climax when push comes to shove. Unknown

To philander is to engage in passing love affairs which, like revolving doors, admit a new girlfriend as the previous one exits. Unknown

A playsuit is a garment that has more play than suit. Unknown

A porno movie is a movie in which the scenery is less important than the obscenery. Unknown

A mistress is a woman who is like a wife, except that she doesn't have to do the dishes. Unknown

Quotes on Sex, Love & Marriage

Nudity has taken all the romance out of semi-nudity. Gregory Nunn

The best mannered people make the most absurd lovers. Denis Diderot

An optimist is a girl who mistakes a bulge for a curve. Ring Lardner

All lovers swear more performance than they are able. Shakespeare

When a man says he had pleasure with a woman he does not mean conversation. Samuel Johnson

One is never entirely without the instinct of looking around. Walt Whitman

A man of fifty looks as old as Santa Claus to a girl of twenty. William Feather

Ejaculation is the upshot of an orgasm. Unknown

Erotomania is an excessive sexual drive where there's no difference between temptation and opportunity. Unknown

An eyebrow pencil is a pencil used by women to draw a man's attention. Unknown

Quotes on Sex, Love & Marriage

A fashion model is a beautiful girl who can wear almost anything or almost nothing. Unknown

A flirt is the woman who can say more in a look than a man can in a book. Unknown

An eunuch is a man cut out to be a bachelor. Unknown

To be intimate with a foolish friend is like going to bed with a razor. Benjamin Franklin

Contempt of sexuality is a crime against life. Friedrich Nietzsche

Don't put off 'till tomorrow what can be enjoyed today. Josh Billings

Next to the pleasure of making a new mistress is that of being rid of an old one. William Wycherley

Insomnia is what a man sometimes gets from the girl who looks like a dream. Unknown

A love nest is a place where a beautiful but dumb girl is kept beautifully and quietly. Unknown

A mistress is a cutie on the q.t. Unknown

A sexpot is a girl or woman whose sex appeal makes feminine capital out of masculine interest. Unknown

Quotes on Sex, Love & Marriage

Sexual intercourse is a matter of free love for the amateur, and fee love for the professional. Unknown

A slut is a woman of lose habits who usually wears tight clothes. Unknown

Smut is merely mentioning the unmentionable. Unknown

A sophisticate is a man who never judges by appearances because many a girl nowadays is as old as her mother looks. Unknown

Shape is what a bathing suit has after a beautiful girl puts it on. Unknown

A mistress is a person halfway between a mister and a mattress. Unknown

The love nest is the place where the girl who offers no resistance leads a very nice existence. Unknown

A model is the girl who shapes her financial career around a good figure. Unknown

A bikini is a beach suit especially made to help a woman get out in the open. Unknown

A topless dancer is an entertainer who tries to make it to the top by wearing clothes that don't. Unknown

Quotes on Sex, Love & Marriage

A whore is a loose woman on the loose. Unknown

A woman is a person who wears a sweater to accentuate the positive, and a girdle to abbreviate the negative. Unknown

We have yet to see a woman marrying a male nitwit because of his big bust. Unknown

Chasing pretty girls never hurt anybody, trouble comes after you catch them. Unknown

Short skirts tend to make men more polite. Did you ever see a man get on a bus ahead of one? Unknown

I liked the topless waitresses. I could have glanced all night. Unknown

Don't worry about avoiding temptation, as you grow older it starts avoiding you. Farmer's Almanac

Liz had a friend named Betsy
Who thought she was really sexy
But all the boys dating her were a bore
Wanting only one thing became a chore
So Liz asked Betsy for a simple kiss
Now Liz and Betsy know sweet bliss. Robert Williams

Love is like sweet nectarine, good to the last drop. Fortune Cookie Wisdom

Quotes on Sex, Love & Marriage

A bikini is a garment that leaves nothing to the imagination, except why it is so expensive. Unknown

A model is a girl who, as long as she watches her figure, has others watch it. Unknown

Sex education may be a good idea in the schools, but I don't think they should be given homework. Bill Cosby

Perfume is any smell that is used to drown a worse one. Elbert Hubbard

Ejaculation is short prayers darted up to God on emergency occasions. Thomas Fuller

Good sex is like good bridge. If you don't have a good partner, you'd better have a good hand. Mae West

A terrible thing happened again last night - nothing. Phyllis Diller

Advice is something that is found in bed. Danish Proverb

I always found that the woman with whom I was in love smelled good; the more profuse her sweat, the sweeter it was to me. G. Casanova

She was short on intellect but long on shape. George Ade

Quotes on Sex, Love & Marriage

A henpecked husband is one who is afraid to tell his pregnant wife that he is sterile. Unknown

A hangover is the bad time that comes from a good time. Unknown

A glamour girl is a fascinating creature that men love to fascinate with. Unknown

Frigidity is the inability of a woman to stomach her husband. Unknown

No woman gets an orgasm from shining the kitchen floor. Betty Friedan

A gold digger is a sexpot with a soft spot for a rumpot with a jackpot. Unknown

Fidelity is something much harder to believe in than infidelity because it can't be proved. Unknown

Some women grow old gracefully, others wear stretch pants. Roger Devlin

The miniskirt is a functional thing. It enables young ladies to run faster, and because of it they have to. John Lindsay

Prostitutes are the highest paid professional women in America. Gail Sheehy

Quotes on Sex, Love & Marriage

In seducing, he who hesitates is a damned fool. Mae West

Many a miss would not be a missus if liquor did not add a spark to her kisses. E.L.C.

Every time a woman leaves off something she looks better, but every time a man leaves off something he looks worse. Will Rogers

A figure is what a girl must keep in order to find a keeper to keep her. Unknown

I used to be a virgin, but I gave it up because there was no money in it. Marsha Warfield

A dirty book gathers no dust. American Proverb

There is nothing a young man can get by wenching but duels, the clap, and bastards. Kathleen Winsor

Beauty's the thing that counts in women; red lips and black eyes are better than brains. Mary J. Elmendorf

One half of the world cannot understand the pleasures of the other. Jane Austen

Graze upon my lips, and when those mounts are dry - stray lower, where the pleasant fountains lie. Gervase Markham

Quotes on Sex, Love & Marriage

A woman reading PLAYBOY feels a little like a Jew reading a Nazi manual. Gloria Steinem

It's a good thing that beauty is only skin deep, or I'd be rotten to the core. Phyllis Diller

I wasn't really naked. I simply didn't have any clothes on. Josephine Baker

Life is like sex. It's not always good, but its always worth trying. Pamela Anderson

Kissing is a means of getting two people so close together that they can't see anything wrong with each other. Rene Yasenek

The difference between pornography and erotica is lighting. Gloria Leonard

When it comes to making love, a girl can always listen faster than a man can talk. Helen Rowland

I'm tired of all this nonsense about beauty being only skin-deep. That's deep enough. What do you want, an adorable pancreas? Jean Kerr

She whose body is young and cool has no need of dancing school. Dorothy Parker

What men call gallantry, and gods adultery, is much more common where the climate's sultry. Lord Byron

Quotes on Sex, Love & Marriage

An unattempted woman cannot boast of her chastity.
Montaigne

It is through the cracks in our brains that ecstasy creeps in.
Logan Pearsall Smith

It is said that passion makes one think in a circle. Oscar Wilde

Better to sit up all night than to go to bed with a dragon.
Jeremy Taylor

Anatomy is something everyone has but it looks better on a girl. Bruce Raeburn

Pleasure is very seldom found where it is sought. Our brightest blazes are commonly kindled by unexpected sparks. Samuel Johnson

Men lose more conquests by their own clumsiness than by any virtue in the woman. Ninon Lenclos

Diseases are the price of ill pleasures. Thomas Fuller

Papa loved mamma
Mamma loved men
Mamma's in the graveyard
Papa's in the pen. Carl Sandburg

Quotes on Sex, Love & Marriage

A woman never forgets her sex. She would rather talk with a man than an angel any day. Oliver Wendell Holmes

A smile is not only woman's best cosmetic but it likewise serves as a non-verbal compliment to her companion. Dr. George W. Crane

The trouble with life is that there are so many beautiful women and so little time. John Barrymore

It's so hard for an old rake to turn over a new leaf. John Barrymore

Marriage has many pains but celibacy has no pleasures. Samuel Johnson

You can't blame nudist for being the way they are, they were born that way. Unknown

An old maid is a debutante who overdid it. Unknown

She had her face lifted, but it fell when she got the bill for repairs. Unknown

Our tastes change as we mature. Little girls like painted dolls; little boys like soldiers. When they grow up, girls like the soldiers and the boys go for the painted dolls. Unknown

Maternity is a matter of fact; paternity a matter of opinion. Unknown

Quotes on Sex, Love & Marriage

About the only thing that comes to him who waits is whiskers. Unknown

Psychologist: a man who, when a good-looking girls enters a room, watches everybody else. Unknown

A good line is the shortest distance between dates. Unknown

Flirt: a girl who got the boy you wanted. Unknown

Sexual pleasure may prove the stimulus and liberator of our finest and most exalted activities. Havelock Ellis

If I told you you have a beautiful body, you wouldn't hold it against me would you? David Fisher

Necessity is the mother of taking chances. Fortune Cookie Wisdom

The more potent a man becomes in the bedroom, the more potent he is in business. Dr. David Reuben

Chastity is a woman's lack of temptation and a man's lack of opportunity. Unknown

Every woman who is not absolutely ugly thinks herself handsome. Lord Chesterfield

Flirting: attention without intention. Unknown

Quotes on Sex, Love & Marriage

I never expected to see the days when girls get sunburned in the places they do now. Will Rogers

Spices can be found in a variety of wives. Frank Dane

Pussy is sweeter than honey and more valuable than money. Mary B. Morrison

Beauty without grace is the hook without the bait. Ralph Waldo Emerson

Beauty will buy no beef. Thomas Fuller

Not every woman in old slippers can manage to look like Cinderella. Don Marquis

A poor beauty finds more lovers than husbands. George Hebert

I always think a bed that hasn't been slept in looks sort of forlorn in the morning. John Van Druten

The bee that hath honey in her mouth, hath a sting in her tail. John Lyly

All that hot stuff that happened in the bible is happening today on every street. Robert Fontaine

You can find women who have had no love affairs, but scarcely any who have had just one. LaRochefoucauld

Quotes on Sex, Love & Marriage

Home is heaven and orgies are vile, but I like an orgy, once in a while. Ogden Nash

A bather whose clothing was strewed
By winds that had left her quite nude,
    Saw a man come along...
    And unless we are wrong,
You thought the next line would be lewd. Unknown

Just as the wolf loves a lamb, so the lover adores his beloved. Plato

What I hate is the girl who gives with a feeling she has to; dry in bed, with her mind somewhere else, gathering wool. Duty is all very well, but let's not confuse it with pleasure! I do not want any girl doing her duty for me. Ovid

The woman who goes to bed with a man should put off her modesty with her skirt and put it on again with her petticoat. Montaigne

Women in love forgive great infidelities more easily than small ones. LaRochefoucauld

A wise woman should never give herself for the first time by appointment, it should be an unforeseen delight. Stendhal

Quotes on Sex, Love & Marriage

With the great majority of animals that taste for the beautiful is confined, as far as we can judge, to the attractions of the opposite sex. Darwin

A cautious young girl from Penzance
Decided to take just one chance.
    She wavered, then lo,
    She let herself go...
Now all of her sisters are aunts. Unknown

Be good, if you can't be good, be careful. Harrington Tate

Adolescence is when Humpty-Dumpty is replaced with hanky-panky. Unknown

I'd rather have two girls at 17 than one at 34. Fred Allen

Whether men will make passes at girls who wear glasses, depends quite a bit on the shape of the chassis. S. Omar Barker

Remember when the air was clean and sex was dirty? Unknown

Business is like sex. When it's good, it's very, very good; when it's not so good, it's still good. Unknown

Of all my relations, I like sex the best. Unknown

Quotes on Sex, Love & Marriage

Helpful hints on how to tip a topless waitress, add up her measurements and give her 2O percent. Unknown

I don't go for topless waitresses, bar maids, shoeshine girls, or topless anything; the best part of getting a present is unwrapping it. Unknown

Sign in a Brassiere Shop: "What God has forgotten - we stuff with cotton." Unknown

A flirt is a woman whose eyes disturb a man's ease. Unknown

A flirt is the girl who cannot get all the men she likes, but likes all the men she can get. Unknown

It was not the apple on the tree, but the pair on the ground, I believe, that caused the trouble in the garden. M.D. O'Connor

If you aren't going all the way, why go at all? Joe Namath

There's nothing wrong with a person's sex life that the right psychoanalyst can't exaggerate. Dr. Laurence Peter

If it is not erotic, it is not interesting. Fernando Arrabal

Sex is the only game not called off on account of darkness. Dr. Laurence Peter

They made love as though they were an endangered species. Peter De Vries

Quotes on Sex, Love & Marriage

Golf is like a love affair: if you don't take it seriously, it's no fun; if you do take it seriously, it breaks your heart. Arnold Daly

How much has to be explored and discarded before reaching the naked flesh of feeling. Claude Debussy

To grow old is to pass from passion to compassion. Albert Camus

In sexual intercourse it's quality not quantity that counts. Dr. David Reuben

A flirt is a girl who winks when she has something in her eye, but more often when she has someone in it. Unknown

A speech is like a love affair. Any fool can start it, but to end it requires considerable skill. Lord Mancroft

What makes resisting temptation difficult, for many people, is that they don't want to discourage it completely. Franklin P. Jones

Good taste and humor are a contradiction in terms, like a chaste whore. Malcom Muggeridge

A flirt is a girl who seems to be throwing herself at a man but is really taking careful aim. Unknown

Quotes on Sex, Love & Marriage

Flirtation is the proof that landing a man is like hooking a fish; it helps to wiggle the bait a little. Unknown

High school is the time when girls start putting on lipstick and the boys start wiping it off. Unknown

A flirt is the woman who attracts a man before marriage and distracts him afterward. Unknown

What kind of nut is the guy who goes to see the topless girls? A chestnut. Unknown

If sex is such a driving force as them scientists say, how come so much of it is always parked? Unknown

Statistics are like a bikini: All that they reveal is important; all that they hide is essential. Unknown

As I was letting down my hair
I met a guy who didn't care;
He didn't care again today-
I love'em when they get that way! Hughes Mearns

Make love to every women you meet; if you get five percent on your outlay, it's a good investment. Arnold Bennett

Nobody wants to kiss when they are hungry. Dorothy Dix

The best letters of our time are those that can never be published. Virginia Wolf

Quotes on Sex, Love & Marriage

Too much of a good thing can be wonderful. Mae West

A kiss on the lips does not always touch the heart. Italian Proverb

Men who do not make advances to women are apt to become victims to women who make advances to them. Walter Bagehot

The trouble with life is that there are so many beautiful women, and so little time. John Barrymore

If she had said "no" just once, I'd not have said another word and left things there, but as she said it more than a dozen times: "No, no, onooo, ooonooo, noooo" - Right! I said to myself; she wants it. Giordano Bruno

Blessed is the wooing that is not long a-doing. Robert Burton

You men are like clocks; you never make love, but you clap your wings, and crow when you have done. John Dryden

The girl with a future avoids a man with a past. Evan Esar

A lover without indiscretion is no lover at all. Thomas Hardy

It is better to love two too many than one too few. Sir John Harington

Quotes on Sex, Love & Marriage

A shoulder strap is a piece of ribbon that keeps an attraction from becoming a sensation. Unknown

She asked me if I knew anything about kissing. Which is rather odd because I was kissing her at the time. Unknown

His kisses were so hot it burned up her husband. Unknown

You can always spot a Peeping Tom at a nudist colony. He's the guy sneaking looks at the girls passing by outside. Unknown

This one woman of ill-repute refuses to admit married men to her house. Her motto is, "I cater to the needy - not the greedy." Unknown

Opportunity knocks, but last night a knock spoiled my opportunity. Unknown

It takes a lot of experience for a girl to kiss like a beginner. Unknown

Before marriage a girl has to kiss her man to hold him, after marriage she has to hold him to kiss him. Unknown

I don't mind girls who kiss and tell, it's good advertising. Unknown

Quotes on Sex, Love & Marriage

A girl who tries to talk her boy friend into buying her a silk nightgown, usually ends up with him trying to talk her out of it. Unknown

Modesty is a relative value; there is the modesty of the woman of twenty, the woman of thirty, the woman of forty-five.
Honore De Balzac

If a man cannot distinguish the difference between the pleasures of two consecutive nights, he has married too early.
Honore De Balzac

One of our unfavorite sights is a mini skirt on a maxi mum.
Harold Coffin

As for women who spend their lives making love, making love is the least of their faults. LaRochefoucauld

He felt as naked as a peeled banana. Frederick Laing

World understanding depends upon people of all nations looking alike, which they cannot do with their clothes on.
Alois Klapp

Love and scandal are the best sweeteners of tea. Henry Fielding

Make two grins grow where there was only a grouch before.
Elbert Hubbard

Quotes on Sex, Love & Marriage

If you want to hide your face, walk naked. Stanislaw J. Lec

A womanizer is a playboy who never makes love to a woman when he has something better to do, but who never finds anything better to do. Unknown

Lately there seems to be an abnormal interest in normal desire. Unknown

The naked truth is the only form of nudity that's not popular today. Unknown

Necking is a form of caress in which the neck is unimportant. Unknown

No is the oldest oral contraceptive. Unknown

A nudist is a girl who loves to run around in her silhouette. Unknown

A nudist camp is where you don't look a person in the face. Unknown

When a man becomes familiar with his goddess, she quickly sinks into a woman. Addison

Statistics are like ladies of the night. Once you get them down, you can do anything with them. Mark Twain

Quotes on Sex, Love & Marriage

Virtue is learned at mother's knee, vices at other joints.
Laurence Peter

A dress that zips up the back will bring a husband and wife together. James Boren

It's time to make love. Douse the glim.
The fireflies flicker and dim.
   The stars lean together
   Like birds of a feather,
And the loin lies down with the limb. Conrad Aiken

Virtue has always been conceived of as victorious resistance to one's vital desire. James Cabell

A nudist camp is the ideal place for the woman who claims she has no clothes to wear. Unknown

A nudist camp is the only place where women wear less than on the beach. Unknown

If sex is such a natural phenomenon why do we need so many books on How To? Apparently nature has a lot to learn from us. Unknown

A beauty contest is like a candy store, everything looks good, but you can't touch. Unknown

Some women show a lot of style and some styles show a lot of women. Unknown

Quotes on Sex, Love & Marriage

The honeymoon is over when a quickie before dinner means a cocktail. Unknown

The popular girl is the one who waxes her zipper to make it work smoothly, silently, and conveniently. Unknown

Men don't love her for her mind, but for what she doesn't mind. Unknown

A womanizer is an amorist who is interested in a good many women, especially if they are not so good. Unknown

It's hard to be funny when you have to be clean. Mae West

When grown-ups do it it's kind of dirty - that's because there's no-one to punish them. Tuesday Weld

My method is basically the same as Masters and Johnson, only they charge thousands of dollars and its called therapy. I charge fifty dollars and it's called prostitution. Xaviera Hollander

Free of her lips--free of her hips. English Proverb

When the cup of any sensual pleasure is drained to the bottom, there is always poison in the dregs. Jane Porter

A philanderer dislikes to be greeted every morning by the sight of the same bra on the back of a chair. Unknown

Quotes on Sex, Love & Marriage

The desire of a man for a woman is not directed at her because she is a human being, but because she is a woman. Kant

This is the monstrosity in love, lady, that the will is infinite and the execution confined, that the desire is boundless and the act a slave to limit. Shakespeare

Our most intense desires are never the mind's alone. LaRochefoucauld

Those who have had great love affairs are forever glad, and forever sorry, that they have ended. LaRochefoucauld

If I had as many love affairs as you fellows have given me credit for, I would now be speaking from inside a jar at the Harvard Medical School. Frank Sinatra

A nudist camp is a summer place where men and women air their differences. Unknown

A nudist colony is a summer resort where women wear the same fashions year after year. Unknown

In the eye of lovers, everything is beautiful. Fortune Cookie Wisdom

Nudity is a person's birthday suit. Unknown

Quotes on Sex, Love & Marriage

It takes mighty little to capture a man's imagination, especially when the right girl is wearing it. Ferris Mack

Kissing a girl is like opening a bottle of olives. If you can get one the rest come easy. Bob Hope

Men seldom jump hurdles for girls who wear girdles. Grady Johnson

The majority of women surrender from weakness rather than passion, wherefore enterprising men, even though not the most attractive, are the most successful. LaRochefoucauld

Here's to our wives and sweethearts; may they never meet. Unknown

Vasectomy means never having to say you're sorry. Unknown

We always shrink from meeting our true love just after we have been dallying elsewhere. LaRochefoucauld

Ladies love to drape their carcasses in gowns bought at Neiman-Marcus's. Lon Tinkle

A woman is to be pitied who is both amorous and chaste. LaRochefoucauld

Man is the only animal that blushes. Or needs to. Mark Twain.

Quotes on Sex, Love & Marriage

A caress is better than a career. Elizabeth Marbury

Its not the men in my life that counts, its the life in my men.
Mae West

A lady is one who never shows her underwear unintentionally.
Unknown

Platonic love: the gun you didn't know was loaded. Unknown

There was a young lady named Rood,
Who was such an absolute prude
   That she pulled down the blind
   When changing her mind
Lest a curious eye should intrude. Unknown

There never was a saint with red hair. Russian Proverb

Strapless gown: a compromise between the law of decency and the law of gravity. Unknown

Europeans used to say Americans were puritanical. Then they discovered that we were not puritans. So now they say we are obsessed with sex. Mary McCarthy

An unattempted woman cannot boast of her chastity.
Montaigne

There are a few things that never go out of style, and a feminine woman is one of them. Jobyna Ralston

Quotes on Sex, Love & Marriage

What I like about masturbation is that you don't have to talk afterwards. Milos Forman

A lady is one who never shows her underwear unintentionally. Lillian Day

The seaside is where a girl rarely bothers to hide her hide. Unknown

The seashore is where many a man's composure is distracted by a woman's exposure. Unknown

The beach is the place where lots of girls invite pursuit by showing lots of girl per suit. Unknown

Beauty is what every girl prefers to brains because every man can see better than he can think. Unknown

A belly dancer is an entertainer who does little more than stand around and twiddle her middle. Unknown

A bikini is the little bit that isn't there. Unknown

A brunette is the girl who didn't follow the instructions on the bottle. Unknown

Chaste is the woman who is seldom chased. Unknown

Quotes on Sex, Love & Marriage

Modern girls wear less clothes on the street than their grandmothers did in bed. Unknown

The only reason I feel guilty about masturbation is that I do it so badly. David Steinberg

If God wanted sex to be fun, He wouldn't have included children as punishment. Ed Bluestone

Football players, like prostitutes, are in the business of ruining their bodies for the pleasure of strangers. Merle Kessler

I can't believe that out of 100,000 sperm, you were the quickest. Steven Pearl

A beautiful and chaste woman is the perfect workmanship of God, the true glory of angels, the rare miracle of earth, and the sole wonder of the world. Hermes

Passions make us feel, but never see clearly. Montesquieu

Trust not too much to an enchanting face. Virgil

The vainest woman is never thoroughly conscious of her beauty till she is loved by the man who sets her own passion vibrating in return. George Eliot

A wink is the light that lies in woman's eyes. Unknown

Quotes on Sex, Love & Marriage

Love with old men is as the sun upon the snow, it dazzles more than it warms them. J.P. Senn

What we learn with pleasure we never forget. Alfred Mercier

Humble wedlock is far better than proud virginity. Augustine

She is adorned amply, that in her husband's eye looks lovely - the truest mirror that an honest wife can see her beauty in. J. Tobin

A wink is a split-second signal and the fastest way to get into trouble. Unknown

A man of pleasure is a man of pains. Young

One half, the finest half of life, is hidden from the man who does not love with passion. Beyle

The worst thing an old man can be is a lover. Otway

A loving maiden grows unconsciously more bold. Richter

Man is an animal which alone among the animals refuses to be satisfied by the fulfillment of animal desires. Alexander Graham Bell

If a mistaken marriage can be purgatory, mistaken celibacy is hell. R.H. Benson

Quotes on Sex, Love & Marriage

Any man may be a celibate who has never had the opportunity to be anything else. Cosmo Hamilton

Everyone has someone to love. Fortune Cookie Wisdom

Neck or nothing. Colley Cibber

Prisons are built with stones of law, brothels with bricks of religion. William Blake

The more one loves one's mistress, the closer one is to hating her. LaRochefoucauld

That woman is one of the Lee sisters, and her first name is Ug. Langston Hughes

Pleasure's a sin and sometimes sin's a pleasure. Lord Byron

A wink is a whether signal. Unknown

A girdle is an elastic device designed to turn your bulges into curves. Unknown

The innocent seldom find an uneasy pillow. Cowper

Beware of her fair locks, for when she winds them around a young man's neck, she will not set him free again. Goethe

A coquette is like a recruiting sergeant, always on the lookout for fresh victims. Jerrold

Quotes on Sex, Love & Marriage

A ballroom is nothing more or less than a great market place of beauty. For my part, were I a buyer, I should like making my purchases in a less public mart. Bulwer

Desires are the pulses of the soul. Manton

A wanton eye is the messenger of an unchaste heart. Augustine

The faces which have charmed us the most escape us the soonest. Walter Scott

There is an evening twilight of the heart, when its wild passion waves are lulled to rest. Halleck

I love a hand that meets my own with a grasp that causes some sensation. F.S. Osgood

It is the strumpet's plague to beguile many, and be beguiled by one. Shakespeare

A girdle is a garment whose difficulty is not the cost, but the upcreep. Unknown

A hooker is a streetwalker who is footloose and fancy, but never free. Unknown

The ideal wife has an old head, a young heart, and a baby face. Unknown

Quotes on Sex, Love & Marriage

Indecisive is the woman who cannot make up her mind how to make up her face. Unknown

Intelligence is what a clever girl hides behind a high hemline and a low neckline. Unknown

A kept women is one who prefers to hold a man's interest rather than his respect. Unknown

A kiss is a trick of nature to stop speech when words become superfluous. Unknown

Kissing is a popular practice where a change of lipstick now and then is relished by philandering men. Unknown

The idealist is the young man who dreams about marrying a beautiful, rich nymphomaniac. Unknown

A woman is a person whose face is her fortune or misfortune. Unknown

A woman is a member of the so-called weaker sex because she has a weakness for the opposite sex. Unknown

Summer is the season when the beaches and bikinis are filled to capacity. Unknown

A miniskirt is a short distance surrounded by long looks. Unknown

Quotes on Sex, Love & Marriage

A miniskirt is a garment that shows up a woman when a woman shows up in it. Unknown

A model is a lassie with a classy chassis. Unknown

A model is a girl whose beautiful figure is shown to advantage by wearing almost anything, or almost nothing. Unknown

A movie star is an actress to whom variety is the spouse of life. Unknown

A chaperone is an old maid who never made the first team, but she's still intercepting passes. Unknown

A wolf is a male animal with two legs and eight hands. Unknown

Only the person who risks is truly free. Fortune Cookie Wisdom

The blush that flies at seventeen is fixed at forty-nine. Rudyard Kipling

Many a good man has caught his death of cold getting up in the middle of the night to go home. Luke McLuke

Some sexes change their sexes now and make a mere man wonder how. Alfred Kreymborg

Quotes on Sex, Love & Marriage

All biological necessities have to be made respectable whether we like it or not. Bernard Shaw

A ship is always referred to as "she" because it costs so much to keep one in paint and powder. Admiral Chester W. Nimitz

The sin is not in the sinning, but in the being found out. W.G. Benham

A slander is like a hornet; if you cannot kill it dead at the first blow, better not strike at it. Josh Billings

Cosmetics are what young women use to improve on Mother Nature, and older women to deceive Father Time. Unknown

A smile increases your face value. Fortune Cookie Wisdom

A bikini is a garment invented so that women could go naked in clothes. Unknown

A bathing beauty is a sight to be held. Unknown

Allure is the quality that enables a beautiful girl to make eyes at you with her whole figure. Unknown

The altogether is the something you're in when you're not in anything else. Unknown

If two be together, then they have heat; how can one be warm alone? The Bible

Quotes on Sex, Love & Marriage

There is no way to catch a snake that is as safe as not catching him. Unknown

The thing in the subway which is called congestion is highly esteemed in the nightclubs as intimacy. Unknown

There was a young lady named Kate,
Who necked in the dark with her date.
    When asked how she fared,
    She said she was scared,
But otherwise doing first-rate. Unknown

When we are weary of love, we welcome infidelity; it absolves us of having to be faithful ourselves. LaRochefoucauld

A blonde is the most dangerous thing to men ever developed by chemistry. Unknown

Teenagers use cosmetics to make them look older sooner, and mothers to make them look younger longer. Unknown

A whore is a deep ditch; and a strange woman is a narrow pit. The Bible

He who looketh upon a woman while driving, loseth a fender. Unknown

If you asked a doctor what you should give the girl who has everything, chances are he'd say, "Penicillin." Unknown

Quotes on Sex, Love & Marriage

Stealing a kiss may be petty larceny but sometimes it's also grand. Unknown

The only kind of letters a woman likes to receive from a man are those which should not have been written. Unknown

Male or female is the first differentiation that you make when you meet another human being, and you are used to making that distinction with absolute certainty. Anatomical science shares your certainty in one point, but not much more. Freud

A kiss that speaks volumes is seldom a first edition. Unknown

Deck thyself now with majesty and excellency; and array thyself with glory and beauty. The Bible

For light, go directly to the source of the light, not any reflections. Fortune Cookie Wisdom

For if we women will but sit at home, powdered and trimmed, clad in our daintiest lawn, employing all our charms, and all our arts to win men's love, and when we've won it, then repel them, firmly, till they end the war, we'll soon get Peace again, be sure of that. Aristophanes

Speak softly and sweetly. Fortune Cookie Wisdom

A toy is an object that makes infancy as interesting to infants as adultery is to adults. Unknown

Quotes on Sex, Love & Marriage

Undress is the sate of being dressed only in your skin.
Unknown

A whistle is a form of flirtation that turns a girl's head.
Unknown

What counts least of all in conventional love-making is love.
LaRochefoucauld

Taking the size of his body into account, man emits more sperm than any other animal. Aristotle

There are few things that we so unwillingly give up, even in advanced age, as the supposition that we still have the power of ingratiating ourselves with the fair sex. Johnson

It was a lover and his lass,
  With a hey, and a ho, and a hey nonino,
That o'er the green corn-field did pass
  In the spring time, the only pretty ring time,
When birds do sing, hey ding a ding, ding:
Sweet lovers love the spring. Shakespeare

The importance of a type of woman for the erotic life of mankind must be recognized as very great. Such women have the greatest fascination for men. Freud

A love affair is an affair between two people who are married, but not to each other. Unknown

Quotes on Sex, Love & Marriage

A flirt is a girl whose favorite man is the next one. Unknown

Buttocks are the bosom of the pants. Unknown

Desire, like a storm, is explosive with creative force. Fortune Cookie Wisdom

A bikini is a bathing suit designed for the nuder gender. Unknown

An actress is a beautiful woman who grows a year older every decade. Unknown

There was a young lady of Oola,
Who waggled her hips in the Hula.
As she dropped her grass skirt,
She cried,'I'm no flirt.
I've stripped to the buff to be coola.' Unknown

It is good for man not to touch a woman. Nevertheless, to avoid fornication, let every man have his own wife, and let every woman have her own husband. The Bible

Adolescence is the age between puberty and adultery. Unknown

A bikini is the suit women wear to outstrip others on the beach. Unknown

Quotes on Sex, Love & Marriage

Our first love and last love is...self love. Fortune Cookie Wisdom

A call girl is one who sends out her mating call over the telephone. Unknown

A flirt is a woman to which every man is worth her wiles. Unknown

A love affair is a happy interlude we always remember, or an unhappy interlude we never forget. Unknown

Nudism is a cult followed by people who were born that way. Unknown

Hope is the best stimulant of life. Fortune Cookie Wisdom

A nudist is the girl who prolongs the life of her bathing suit by taking it off before entering the water. Unknown

A pickup is the woman who is always up to date. Unknown

Makeup powder is the dust that the gods have given to women to blind the eyes of men. Unknown

A shoulder strap is a small piece of ribbon with a large responsibility. Unknown

A showgirl is a creature who is so called because she shows plenty. Unknown

Quotes on Sex, Love & Marriage

You have to whistle at a shy girl twice. Unknown

The bikini is the proof that women need but little here below. Unknown

The swimsuit is the beach fashion for which you pay more money for less clothes. Unknown

A vacation is a holiday in the mountains where a girl can see the scenery, or at the beach where she can be the scenery. Unknown

Virtue is usually a case of insufficient temptation. Unknown

Vulva are the private parts of a chaste woman, or the public parts of a prostitute. Unknown

A bikini is feminine beachwear that has solved the problem of how to conceal and reveal at the same time. Unknown

A showgirl is one who has no more on her mind than anywhere else. Unknown

A pickup is a woman who believes in affair play. Unknown

A nudist is person in a one-button suit. Unknown

A showgirl usually keeps her hair light and her past dark. Unknown

Quotes on Sex, Love & Marriage

A slut is a woman who has been tried and found wanton. Unknown

A star is a word that stands for a heavenly body, or for the woman who has one. Unknown

Strip poker is a game in which the more you lose, the more you have to show for it. Unknown

Summer is the season when the best comic strips are on the beach. Unknown

A sweater is a garment designed to tell the difference between the sexes at a glance. Unknown

A trollop is a girl who can't resist the man who can't resist a girl. Unknown

Virgin is a word derived from the Latin vir, meaning man, and gin, meaning trap; hence a man-trap. Unknown

Virtue is just vice resting while recharging its battery. Unknown

A sweater is a garment that lends sex appeal to some girls, while all it does for others is make them itch. Unknown

Striptease is a performance where the girls all try to outstrip one another. Unknown

Quotes on Sex, Love & Marriage

A showgirl is one who usually has an interesting history and even more interesting geography. Unknown

Dressing is something it takes a woman longer to do than a man because she has to slow down at the curves. Unknown

Adultery is the wrong man in the right place. Unknown

Cheesecake: a magazine with a beautiful girl on the cover-and no cover on the girl. Unknown

A spa is a fashionable establishment whose aim is to turn out thinner sinners. Unknown

A lady is a women who keeps pulling up her strapless gown. Unknown

A virgin is a woman who longs to meet her maker. Unknown

Artificial insemination: copulation without representation. Playboy

The weaker sex is the stronger sex because of the weakness of the stronger sex for the weaker sex. Unknown

A virgin is a maiden who has never lost her head. Unknown

A spa is a slimming resort where a woman deliberately goes out of her weigh to please some man. Unknown

Quotes on Sex, Love & Marriage

Alcohol is a beverage that makes you lose your inhibitions and give exhibitions. Unknown

An affair is the relationship that confuses the feeling of love with the making of love. Unknown

A drive-in theater is an outdoor movie where more happens in the cars than on the screen. Unknown

A siren is a seductive woman who, because she has a way with her, generally has a man with her. Unknown

The swimsuit is the bikini women wear to bare. Unknown

A harlot is a woman who gets more with her thighs than with her sighs. Unknown

Happiness is a perfume you can't pour on others without getting a few drops on yourself. Unknown

Glamorous is the woman who is never overlooked, but always looked over. Unknown

A flirt is never a sweetheart, but always a cheatheart.
Unknown

A fashion model is a girl who shows a lot of style, or whose style shows a lot of girl. Unknown

Quotes on Sex, Love & Marriage

An evening gown is another thing that shows the stuff you're made of. Unknown

Sunstroke is what you get if you make hay while the sun shines. Unknown

A sweater is an outer garment that enables a girl to put up a good front. Unknown

The swimsuit has turned swimming into a spectator sport. Unknown

A suntan is the only thing that sticks closer to a girl than a bathing suit. Unknown

An evening gown is a dress that usually keeps everybody warm but the wearer. Unknown

A flirt is a woman who notices a man in such a way that he notices her. Unknown

A swimsuit is the difference between decent and indecent exposure. Unknown

A woman will look spic in slacks if she hasn't too much span. Unknown

Sex is a mutual fun investment. Unknown

Sex is the most popular form of physical exercises. Unknown

Quotes on Sex, Love & Marriage

There is a boundary to men's passions when they act from feeling; but none when they are under the influence of imagination. Edmund Burke

Illusion is the first of all pleasures. Voltaire

Most women caress sin before embracing penitence. Bernard Fontenelle

There are worse occupations in this world than feeling a woman's pulse. Laurence Sterne

Sex is the most fun you can have without laughing. Unknown

Sex is the proof that the nearest way to one's heart is not always through the stomach. Unknown

A sexagenarian is a man with more sex in his age than in his urge. Unknown

A sexagenarian is a person whose thoughts turn from passion to pension. Unknown

Sex appeal is what a bikini takes on when there's a girl in it. Unknown

A man in passion rides a mad horse. Benjamin Franklin

Quotes on Sex, Love & Marriage

Play with an ass and he will wag his tail in your face. Jacob Cats

The woman tempted me-and tempts me still!
Lord God, I pray You that she ever will! Edmund Vance Cooke

Enjoy yourself while you can. Fortune Cookie Wisdom

Never play cards with a man called Doc. Never eat at a place called Mom's. Never sleep with a woman whose troubles are worse than your own. Nelson Algren

Sex appeal is the allure that evaporates when the sweater is a little too large. Unknown

Sex education is a course of study whose best part is the homework. Unknown

Sex education is something that sometimes starts in the home, but more often in the driveway. Unknown

A stripper is a girl who never puts off till tomorrow what she can take off today. Unknown

A stripteaser is an underpaid performer who makes a bare living. Unknown

Quotes on Sex, Love & Marriage

A prude is one who blushes modestly at the indelicacy of her thoughts and virtuously flies from the temptation of her desires. Ambrose Bierce

My advice to women's clubs of America is to raise more hell and fewer dahlias. James McNeill Whistler

Plain women are always jealous of their husbands, beautiful women never are; they have no time, they are always occupied in being jealous of other people's husbands. Oscar Wilde

A good folly is worth whatever you pay for it. George Ade

The girl who makes the poet's sigh is a very different creature from the girl who makes his soup. Frederick Cheldon

Fidelity: a virtue peculiar to those who are about to be betrayed. Ambrose Bierce

A woman will flirt with anybody in the world as long as other people are looking on. Oscar Wilde

Kissing don't last, cookery do. George Meredith

Summer is the time of year when girls have stockinged legs that look bare or bare legs that look stockinged. Unknown

A sweater is a garment that brings out the bust in a woman. Unknown

Quotes on Sex, Love & Marriage

A stripteaser is an entertainer whose clothes are so designed that she is always seen in the best places. Unknown

A strumpet is the girl who knows more sailors than an admiral. Unknown

Strip poker is a game that's always good to the last drop. Unknown

A smile is nature's way to improve your looks. Unknown

A sinner is one who prefers to have something to remember than nothing to regret. Unknown

Sexology is the only study of human behavior where the beginner starts in the middle. Unknown

A sexpot is an erotic creature whose body has gone to her head. Unknown

A sexpot is a female who uses her physical curves as an angle to attract men. Unknown

Sheer is the nearest thing to nothing, and prettier in black. Unknown

A strapless gown is one that is down to see level. Unknown

A woman never forgets her sex. She would rather talk to a man than an angel any day. Oliver Wendell Holmes

Quotes on Sex, Love & Marriage

If a woman hasn't got a tiny streak of a harlot in her, she's a dry stick as a rule. D.H. Lawrence

Whether they give or refuse, it delights a woman to have been asked. Ovid

Ladies, like soldiers, ought to keep their powder dry before going into action. Horace Syndham

Listen to life, and you will hear the voice of life crying. Be! Fortune Cookie Wisdom

It is one of the mysterious ways of Allah to make women troublesome when he makes them beautiful. Bernard Shaw

If you think you love your mistress for her own sake, you are quite mistaken. LaRochefoucauld

A strapless gown is kept up by a woman's sense of decency or by a city ordinance. Unknown

A streetwalker is a poor woman in seduced circumstances. Unknown

In ancient mythology a nymph was a beautiful maiden who could feel perfectly happy without owning a stitch of clothes. Unknown

Quotes on Sex, Love & Marriage

A nymphet is a sexually precocious girl who has evolved from pigtails to cocktails. Unknown

A nympho is a woman who can do without men but not for long. Unknown

Nymphomania is the erotic desire of a woman to love too much, and too many. Unknown

Nymphomania is a compulsive disorder where the patient has a repeated need to be bedridden. Unknown

One cannot know the best that is in him. Fortune Cookie Wisdom

Nymphomania is an uncontrollable drive by a woman not to give all to love, but to give love to all. Unknown

Nymphomania is the abnormal feminine drive to engage in love affairs, not merely letting it happen but helping it happen. Unknown

A nymphomaniac is a woman with a constant surge in the urge to merge. Unknown

Luck sometimes visits a fool, but it never sits down with him. Fortune Cookie Wisdom

A nymphomaniac is a woman who will go to bed with a man right after she has come from the beauty parlor. Unknown

Quotes on Sex, Love & Marriage

Obscenity is a word that cannot be defined accurately without using obscene words. Unknown

An old maid is the woman who failed to strike while the iron was hot. Unknown

An orgy is group therapy. Unknown

A penis is another thing that comes in like a lion and goes out like a lamb. Unknown

Perfume is a bottled mating call. Unknown

Petting is the study of anatomy in braille. Unknown

Petting is what some girls go in for and what others go out for. Unknown

She got her good looks from her father - he's a plastic surgeon. Groucho Marx

Of all the delights of this world man cares most for sexual intercourse, yet he has left it out of his heaven. Mark Twain

When a woman hires a detective to follow her husband, it's probably to learn what the other woman sees in him. Dr. Laurence Peter

Quotes on Sex, Love & Marriage

Let us have wine and women, mirth and laughter; Sermons and soda water the day after. Lord Byron

A vasectomy is never having to say you're sorry. Rubin Carson

Middle age is when you change from a stud to a dud. Dr. Laurence Peter

Petting is to fondle intimately, like the proverbial virgin on the verge. Unknown

Phallus is the male sexual organ that comes in three conditions: docile, fossil, and colossal. Unknown

A girl wears a girdle to take her in so a man will take her out. Unknown

A streetwalker is a prostitute who is inclined to wear out more sheets than shoes. Unknown

A stripper is a girl who has nothing to wear, and wears it. Unknown

A stripper is a girl who wears more clothes in bed than at work. Unknown

A stripper is the only girl who feels overdressed in an bikini. Unknown

Quotes on Sex, Love & Marriage

Strip poker is the only game that can't be played at a nudist camp. Unknown

Striptease is a show where the performer doesn't read her lines, but shows them. Unknown

Striptease is a performance where the audience applauds the entertainer more and more for less and less. Unknown

A sweater is a garment whose right size for a girl is the tight size. Unknown

A sweater is a garment worn by a girl to pull men's eyes over the wool. Unknown

A swimsuit is a form of semifeminudity. Unknown

A swimsuit is a bikini that women seem to get the most out of. Unknown

A swimsuit is a beach garment that holds fast going around the curves. Unknown

Promiscuity is going out on a lark and ending up in some bird's nest. Unknown

Promiscuity is the intimate relation between two persons, sometimes involving affection but more often infection. Unknown

Quotes on Sex, Love & Marriage

A prostitute is a woman who hates poverty worse than sin. Unknown

Prostitution is a trade where a woman turns her pubic area into a public area. Unknown

A prude is one who always thinks below the belt. Unknown

It is not easy to be a pretty woman without causing mischief. Anatole Franc

There are no ugly women; there are only women who do not know how to look pretty. Jean Bruyere

Fidelity bought with money can be overcome with money. Seneca

Man is the only animal that blushes. Or needs to. Mark Twain.

Passion often turns the cleverest men into idiots and makes the greatest blockheads clever. LaRochefoucauld

A man is as old as he's feeling, a woman as old as she looks. Martimer Collins

Get to the point and keep it clear and simple. Fortune Cookie Wisdom

Quotes on Sex, Love & Marriage

The age of a woman doesn't mean a thing. The best tunes are played on the oldest fiddles. Sigmund Engel

No disguise can long conceal love where it exists, or long feign it where it is lacking. LaRochefoucauld

The thing that takes up the least amount of time and causes the most amount of trouble is sex. John Barrymore

A prude is a girl who no's what her date is up to. Unknown

Being prudish is getting most of your pleasure from being shocked by other people's pleasures. Unknown

Public opinion is the only thing more fickle than a flirt. Unknown

A pushover is an easy mark who allows herself to be handled more than a ketchup bottle at a truck stop. Unknown

A sensualist is one who does not enjoy the chase unless he eats the game. Unknown

A sensualist is the lusty young man who doesn't know when to stop until he is told where to go. Unknown

In matters of love and appetite beware of surfeits. Nothing contributes so much to the duration of either as moderation in their gratification. Bovee

Quotes on Sex, Love & Marriage

As love increases, prudence diminishes. Rochefoucauld

We lose the peace of years when we hunt after the rapture of moments. Bulwer

If you would not step into the harlot's house, do not go by the harlot's door. Secker

Inconstancy is but a name to fright poor lovers from a better choice. Rutter

The nurse of infidelity is sensuality. Cecil

Who has a daring eye, tells downright truths and downright lies. Lavater

It is the passion that is in a kiss that gives to it its sweetness; it is the affection in a kiss that sanctifies it. Bovee

Stolen kisses are always sweetest. Leigh Hunt

Once he drew, with one long kiss, my whole soul through my lips. Tennyson

A man's best friends are his ten fingers. Robert Collyer

A sensualist is a man whose chief interest is not the women in his life but the life in his women. Unknown

Quotes on Sex, Love & Marriage

Sensuality is the reason why it's not the coldest girl who gets the mink coat. Unknown

Stockings are something that's well-filled by Santa Claus but better filled by Mother Nature. Unknown

A pickup is a winked victory. Unknown

A pickup is a young woman who is too impatient to wait for an introduction. Unknown

Comparative anatomy is the most popular course of study on spring break. Unknown

Cosmetics are proof that beauty is only skin deep. Unknown

We have been God-like in our planned breeding of our domesticated plants and animals, but we have been rabbit-like in our unplanned breeding of ourselves. Arnold Toynbee

A correspondence course of passion was, for her, the perfect and ideal relationship with a man. Aldous Huxley

Unless a woman has an amorous heart, she is a dull companion. Samuel Johnson

Passions are vices or virtues in their highest powers. Goethe

Pleasure is like a frail dewdrop, while it laughs it dies.
Rabindranath Tagore

Quotes on Sex, Love & Marriage

There is no such thing as pure pleasure; some anxiety always goes with it. Ovid

It is illegal in England to state in print that a wife can and should derive sexual pleasure from intercourse. Bertrand Russell

Cosmetics is the price the male has to pay for the beauty of the female. Unknown

A woman wears makeup so that her face won't wear off as the evening wears on. Unknown

Dancing is hugging set to music. Unknown

A decollete is a dress with a neckline low enough to make a baby cry. Unknown

A dimple is a small hollow in each cheek to tack a smile in place. Unknown

The word distract means to draw attention away, like the woman who distracts attention from her big feet by wearing a low neckline. Unknown

An evening gown is a dress that is often attractive, but more often distractive. Unknown

Quotes on Sex, Love & Marriage

A fair face may fade, but a beautiful soul last forever. Fortune Cookie Wisdom

An evening gown is the dress a woman wears to be seen in the best places. Unknown

Most women are not so young as they are painted. Max Beerbohm

God has given you one face, and you make yourself another. William Shakespeare

Her face was her chaperone. Rupert Hughes

Prostitution is a market where you can buy grunts and groans that are supposed to sound like love. Wayland Young

In Spain lust is in the air. There is nothing clandestine about the Spanish appreciation of sex, nothing inhibited or restrained. That is why there are very few sexual crimes in Spain. Fernando Diaz-Plaja

With worrying about getting someone pregnant and the AIDS epidemic, having sex today is like having both your balls loaded for bear and playing Russian Roulette with your pecker. Robert Williams

A bed is love's theater. Honore de Balzac

Quotes on Sex, Love & Marriage

An evening gown is the dress designed to help it's wearer catch a man or a cold. Unknown

Why does a blind man's wife paint herself? Benjamin Franklin

Life without vanity is almost impossible. Leo Tolstoy

Be virtuous and you will be eccentric. Mark Twain

Much wanting makes many a maid wanton. Maxwell Anderson

A woman that paints puts up a bill that she is to let. Thomas Fuller

The puritan strain in our culture hounded the professional out of the brothel and forced her to move into the apartment next door, where she quickly became the best tenant. Harry Golden

That a man of intellect has doubts about his mistress is conceivable, but about his wife!-that would be too stupid. Honore De Balzac

It is harder for women to control their coquetry than their passion. LaRochefoucauld

An exhibitionist is a sexy girl who seeks to reveal what others conceal. Unknown

Quotes on Sex, Love & Marriage

An exhibitionist is a person who is not ashamed of anything except of being ashamed. Unknown

A pickup is a meeting of strangers who first talk about the weather and then about whether. Unknown

A plunging neckline is another thing that ruins a man's memory for faces. Unknown

Popular is the girl who lives a date-to-date existence. Unknown

The population explosion is the continuing increase is population due to the continuing increase in copulation. Unknown

A porno movie is a movie that has turned sex into a spectator sport. Unknown

A painter who has the feel of breasts and buttocks is saved. Auguste Renoir

When the candles are out all women are fair. Plutarch

Every girl should use what Mother Nature gave her before Father Time takes it away. Laurence J. Peter

A Canadian is somebody who knows how to make love in a canoe. Pierre Berton

Quotes on Sex, Love & Marriage

What kills a skunk is the publicity it gives itself. Abraham Lincoln

No matter how much cats fight, there always seem to be plenty of kittens. Abraham Lincoln

Some cheat by not cheating. Baltasar Gracian

Absence extinguishes small passions and increases great ones, as the wind will blow out a candle, and blow in a fire. La Rochefoucauld

Girls are something old men love for what they are, and young men for what they promise to be. Johann Goethe

I prefer an interesting vice to a virtue that bores. Moliere,,

A porno movie goes from bed to worse. Unknown

So they came into that bed so steadfast, loved of old, opening glad arms to one another. Homer

A married woman ought not be like any chance female when the light is out. It is when her body is invisible that her virtue and her sole devotion and affection for her husband should be evident. Plutarch

Wives may be merry, and yet honest too. Shakespeare

Quotes on Sex, Love & Marriage

Our connections with the fair sex are founded on the pleasure of enjoyment; on the happiness of loving and being loved; and likewise on the ambition of pleasing the ladies. Montesquieu

A bathing beauty is a pretty girl with an alluring figure who looks tempting in anything - or nothing. Unknown

There can only be one end to marriage without love, and that is love without marriage. John Collins

A chap ought to save a few of the long evenings he spends with his girl till after they're married. Kin Hubbard

Many a man has fallen in love with a girl in a light so dim he would not have chosen a suit by it. Maurice Chevalier

It is only with scent and silk and artifices that we raise love from an instinct to a passion. George Moore

A bathing beauty is a girl with a lovely profile all the way down. Unknown

A bathing suit is a garment that designers shortened first from the bottom, then from the top, and finally from the middle. Unknown

A woman can keep a first lover very long if she does not take a second. LaRochefoucauld

Quotes on Sex, Love & Marriage

A porno movie is a type of entertainment that has to be sin to be appreciated. Unknown

Pregnancy is infanticipation. Unknown

A pickup is a female who may not be equal to the occasion, but is always equal to the occasional. Unknown

A lecher is the philanderer who, having tried them both, believes there's no difference between fornication and adultery . Unknown

A lesbian is a women to whom sex is not procreational, but recreational. Unknown

Lesbianism is the love of bosom buddies. Unknown

Lewd is a four - letter word applied to other four - letter words by people who find them offensive. Unknown

Lipstick is a modern object that lends new flavor to an old pastime. Unknown

No man is so virtuous as to marry only to have children.
Martin Luther

A woman is as old as she looks to a man that likes to look at her. Peter Dunne

Quotes on Sex, Love & Marriage

Rare are those who prefer virtue to the pleasures of sex. Confucius

If ever you are in doubt as to whether or not you should kiss a pretty girl, always give her the benefit of the doubt. Thomas Carlyle

If men knew all that women think, they'd be twenty times more daring. Alphonse Karr

Man only has two primal passions, to get and to beget. Sir William Osler

She laughs at everything you say. Why? Because she has fine teeth. Benjamin Franklin

A lover teaches a wife all her husband kept hidden from her. Honore de Balzac

Lipstick is a cosmetic that a girl can't keep on, and a man can't wipe off. Unknown

Love is a funny feeling that causes a man to bite a girl's neck because she has beautiful legs. Unknown

A love affair is an illicit affair that was formerly called sin, but is nowadays called experience. Unknown

A love nest is usually the private number of a public figure. Unknown

Quotes on Sex, Love & Marriage

Masturbation is a handy expedient in the absence of a partner.
Unknown

Quotes on Sex, Love & Marriage

Quotes on Love & Romance

In a Maui discotheque: "Not responsible for dates left over ten minutes." Unknown

Paranoid is the couple interrupted by a cop in lover's lane. Unknown

What is youth except a man or woman before it is fit to be seen? Evelyn Waugh

Coffee should be black as Hell, strong as death, and sweet as love. Turkish Proverb

God can heal a broken heart, but He has to have all the pieces. Fortune Cookie Wisdom

Old birds are hard to pluck. German Proverb

Of all sexual aberrations, chastity is the strangest. Anatole France

Love laughs at locksmiths. Unknown

It is never considered quite nice
To make passes at ladies twice.
It is clumsy and crude
And exceedingly rude;
Besides, usually once will suffice. Unknown

Quotes on Sex, Love & Marriage

A wolf is a man with a little black book of canceled chicks. Playboy

A man will often take a girl to some retreat in order to make advances. Playboy

The man who wouldn't be a fool over the right woman doesn't deserve to have the right woman be a fool over him. Unknown

It is better to be made a fool of by women than to be ignored by them. Unknown

Never come crawling to a man for love. He likes to get a run for his money. Mae West

Platonic friendship: the interval between the introduction and the first kiss. Sophie Irene Loeb

I miss you when something good happens, because you're the one I want to share it with. I miss you when something is troubling me, because you're the one that understands me so well. I miss you when I laugh and cry, because I know that you are the one that makes my laughter grow and my tears disappear. I miss you all the time, but I miss you the most when I lay awake at night, and think of all the wonderful times that we spent with each other for those were some of the best and most memorable times of my life. Unknown

Quotes on Sex, Love & Marriage

The loves of some people are but the results of good suppers.
Nicholas Chamfort

Marriage is a trick to give a man's sweetheart of today an advantage over his sweetheart of tomorrow. Unknown

Matrimony is the only foolproof way to find out what the man you love really thinks of you. Unknown

Love is composed of a single soul inhabiting two bodies.
Aristotle

A modern novel is from cover to cover, a story than runs from lover to lover. Unknown

The moon is the celestial body that affects the tide and the untied. Unknown

To love is to admire with the heart; to admire is to love with the mind. Theophile Gautier

Being deeply loved by someone gives you strength, while loving someone deeply gives you courage. Lao Tzu

Some people feel with their heads and think with their hearts.
G.C. Lichtenberg

Any kiddies in school can love like a fool, but hating, my boy, is an art. Ogden Nash

Quotes on Sex, Love & Marriage

You know you're in love when you can't fall asleep because reality is finally better than your dreams. Dr. Seuss

Friendship may, and often does, grow into love; but love never subsides into friendship. Lord Byron

Love is the thing that makes the heart light and the parlor dark. Unknown

Love is when you look into someone's eyes and you see their heart. Unknown

The best way to hold a man is in your arms. Unknown

You know a boy is growing up when he stops wanting to go out with girls and wants to stay home with them. Unknown

A morning text doesn't only mean "Good Morning". It has a silent, loving message that says: "I think of you when I wake up". Unknown

Love is an irresistible desire to be irresistibly desired. Robert Frost

Girl to soon-to-be ex-boyfriend: "Let me explain it to you this way, if our romance was on TV, I'd be switching channels." Unknown

Tears are the safety-valve of the heart when too much pressure is laid on it. Albert Smith

Quotes on Sex, Love & Marriage

Love is loveliest when embalmed in tears. Walter Scott

Two people in love, alone, isolated from the world, that's beautiful. Milan Kundera

What a hell of witchcraft lies in the small orb of one particular tear! Shakespeare

Love is like a flower - you've got to let it grow. John Lennon

He soft soaped her until she couldn't see for the suds. Mary Roberts Rinehart

Great hate follows great love. Irish Proverb

Because someone doesn't love you the way you want them to, doesn't mean they don't love you with all they have. Unknown

Scratch a lover and find a foe. Dorothy Parker

I have found the paradox, that if you love until it hurts, there can be no more hurt, only more love. Mother Teresa

Love is like hash, you have to have confidence in it to enjoy it. Unknown

Many a young couple who have nothing in common fool around until they do. Unknown

Quotes on Sex, Love & Marriage

The great secrets of being courted, are, to shun others, and to seem delighted with yourself. Bulwer

To love is to place our happiness in the happiness of another. Leibnitz

If we do not change direction, we are likely to end up where we are headed. Fortune Cookie Wisdom

The reason why lovers are never weary of one another is this - they are always talking of themselves. Rochefoucauld

Love looks not with the eyes, but with the mind, And therefore is winged Cupid painted blind. William Shakespeare

We attract hearts by the qualities we display: we retain them by the qualities we possess. Suard

Sex is always about emotions. Good sex is about free emotions; bad sex is about blocked emotions. Deepak Chopra

A bachelor comes to work from a different direction each morning. Unknown

Don't wait for your ship to come in, swim out to it. Fortune Cookie Wisdom

Any girl who says she'll go through anything for a man usually has his bank book in mind. Unknown

Quotes on Sex, Love & Marriage

The salesgirl at the perfume counter leaned over toward her young customer and warned: "Let me give you a word of advise, don't use this if you're bluffing." Unknown

He who kisses and runs away will live to kiss another. Unknown

People think your soul mate is your perfect fit. And that's what everyone wants. But a true soul mate is a mirror, the person who shows you everything that is holding you back, the person who brings you to your own attention so you can change your life. Elizabeth Gilbert

Some girls are music lovers, others can love without it. Unknown

A husband is a lover who pushed his luck too far. Unknown

A wallflower is a girl whose ambition is to grow on a man. Unknown

Love is your pain in my heart. Unknown

She's at the age where any man who looks back, looks good. Unknown

A cheapskate tries to make every dollar go farther, and every girl too. Unknown

All the world loves a lover, except the husband. Unknown

Quotes on Sex, Love & Marriage

Pure love is a willingness to give without a thought of receiving anything in return. Fortune Cookie Wisdom

If you want proof that girls are dynamite, just try to drop one. Unknown

Every man likes to see a broad smile, especially if broad she smile at him. Unknown

A wallflower is a girl whose romances have been nipped in the bud. Unknown

A wolf is a guy who is always in there pinching. Unknown

The only whole heart is one that has been broken at least once. Unknown

Just because some fool came into your life and lied and cheated on you doesn't mean the next person will too. Don't make everyone pay for what happened in your past. I know it's hard right now, but if you ever want to find love again, you're got to open your heart and let someone in. Karen Kostyla

A wallflower is a girl who usually goes to seed before getting picked. Unknown

The most delicate, the most sensible of all pleasures, consists in promoting the pleasure of others. Bruyere

Quotes on Sex, Love & Marriage

The sweetest of all sounds is that of the voice of the woman we love. Bruyere

Lover's vows seem sweet in every whispered word. Byron

It is in learning music that many youthful hearts learn to love. Ricard

Music is the medicine of the breaking heart. A. Hunt

The heart of a young woman in love is a golden sanctuary which often enshrines an idol of clay. Limayrac

Tenderness is greater proof of love than the most passionate of vows. Marlene Dietrich

Kissing your hand may make you feel very good but a diamond bracelet lasts forever. Anita Loos

If you love something, set it free..if it returns keep it and love it forever. Fortune Cookie Wisdom

Heaven will not be heaven to me if I do not meet my wife there. Andrew Jackson

To womanize is to be constantly in love but not constant in love. Unknown

To womanize is being ever ready to give up a passing fancy for something fancier. Unknown

Quotes on Sex, Love & Marriage

A womanizer is a sensualist whose business is always picking up. Unknown

A womanizer is a man who believes in enduring love, provided he doesn't have to endure it too long. Unknown

To woo is to pursue a girl who is running toward you. Unknown

To woo is what many a young man does without being careful enough in his choice of mother-in-law. Unknown

My daughter is waiting for the right man to come along, but in the meantime she's keeping in practice with the wrong ones. Unknown

A hug is a roundabout way of making love. Unknown

A sweetheart is a girl whose dinner costs a man much more than his wife's. Unknown

A sweetheart is a girl who steals, lies and swears; steals into your arms, lies there, and swears she will never love another. Unknown

A triangle is a love affair involving three persons that usually ends in a wreck-tangle. Unknown

Quotes on Sex, Love & Marriage

What you do with sincerity pays the greatest reward. Fortune Cookie Wisdom

A triangle is a situation when what a woman dislikes most about her husband is another woman. Unknown

Unlucky is the man who makes a blind date and winds up with his own wife. Unknown

Wile is the feminine art of winning domestic arguments by a few tears and sniffles. Unknown

A window shade is a device invented because, while love is blind, the neighbors aren't. Unknown

A wink takes only a second to do, but sometimes a lifetime to undo. Unknown

A woman is the female who is either a hit or a miss. Unknown

A triangle is a group of three people, two of whom fool around with love as if it weren't loaded. Unknown

A romance is something made up largely of red roses and white lies. Unknown

A romance is a mutual meeting of feelings that turns into a mutual meeting of minds. Unknown

Quotes on Sex, Love & Marriage

A romance is a courtship during which a girl usually whines a man around her finger. Unknown

Love reckons hours for months, and days for years; and every little absence is an age. Dryden

Flowers are love's truest language. P. Benjamin

To love and be loved is the greatest happiness of existence. Sydney Smith

Our affections are our life. We live by them; they supply our warmth. Channing

The flame of anger, bright and brief, sharpens the barb of love. W.S. Landor

Hell is not to love anymore. George Bernanos

Of all earthly music that which reaches furthest into heaven is the beating of a truly loving heart. H.W. Beecher

A romance is a love affair that turns a reliable man into as big a liar as the rest of us. Unknown

We pardon as long as we love. Rochefoucauld

A romance is a love affair where we enjoy not so much the gift of the lover as the love of the giver. Unknown

Quotes on Sex, Love & Marriage

A romance is a courtship that often begins by a splashing fountain and ends over a leaky faucet. Unknown

The ability to make love frivolously is the chief characteristic which distinguishes human beings from the beasts. Heywood Broun

The heart of a woman is never so full of affection that there does not remain a little corner for flattery and love. Mauvaux

First love is an instinct, at once a gift and a sacrifice. Every other is a philosophy, a bargain. A.S. Hardy

Our first love, and last love is self-love. Bovee

Love reasons without reason. Shakespeare

Love is a canvas furnished by Nature and embroidered by imagination. Voltaire

Nuptial love maketh mankind; friendly love perfecteth it; but wanton love corrupteth and embaseth it. Bacon

A romance is something anticipated with pleasure, experienced with problems, and remembered with nostalgia. Unknown

A romance is the short period when a couple are deeply in love, followed by a long period when they are deeply in debt. Unknown

Quotes on Sex, Love & Marriage

Heaven has no rage like love to hatred turned. Congreve

Something is wrong here: sex has been with us since the human race began its existence, yet I would estimate that 90 percent of human beings still suffer enormous inhibitions in this area. Xaviera Hollander

There is no instinct like that of the heart. Byron

The heart is an astrologer that always divines the truth. Calderon

Heav'n is but the vision of fulfilled desire. And hell the shadow from a soul on fire. Omar Khayyam

The adoration of his heart had been to her only as the perfume of a wild flower, which she had carelessly crushed with her foot in passing. Longfellow

All loving emotions, like plants, shoot up most rapidly in the tempestuous atmosphere of life. Richter

A lover's eyes will gaze an eagle blind. Shakespeare

A teaser is a girl who in fishing for a man fishes merely for the sport. Unknown

Sex at age 90 is like trying to shoot pool with a rope. George Burns

Quotes on Sex, Love & Marriage

Temperamental is loving a man because you hate him and laughing because you are crying about it. Unknown

Tennis is another game in which love means nothing. Unknown

A teaser is the flirt with a wink and stare of whom men should beware, since she fools every man who expects an affair. Unknown

The eyes are the pioneers that first announce the soft tale of love. Propertius

A romance is a love affair when love makes a man want a girl just as she is, while a girl wants to altar his status. Unknown

Remember when atmospheric contaminants were romantically called stardust? Lane Olinghouse

Faults are thick where love is thin. James Howell

Puppy love is the only thing that can get a boy to wash his neck and ears. Unknown

A pushover is a girl who is easy to get but hard to take. Unknown

A romance is anything that ends in a wedding. Unknown

Quotes on Sex, Love & Marriage

A youth with his first cigar makes himself sick; a youth with his first girl makes other people sick. Mary Wilson Little

If love makes the world go 'round, why are we going to outer space? Margaret Gilman

In nine cases out of ten a women had better show more affection than she feels. Jane Austen

Love is like the moon; when it does not increase it decreases. Segur

There is nothing half so sweet in life as love's young dream. Moore

Love is love's reward. Dryden

In jealousy there is more of self-love, than of love to another. Rochefoucauld

Love is as necessary to human beings as food and shelter. Fortune Cookie Wisdom

A spinster is a bachelor's wife. Unknown

Praise a wife but remain a bachelor. Italian Proverb

If a man is highly sexed he's virile.
If a woman is, she's a nymphomaniac.
With them it's power

Quotes on Sex, Love & Marriage

but with us it's a disease!
Even the act of sex is called penetration!
Why don't they call it enclosure?   Gemma Hatchback

Only little boys and old men sneer at love. Louis Auchincloss

As soon as you cannot keep anything from a woman, you love her. Paul Geraldy

Osculation is an act of affection that brings two lovers so close together that they can't see anything wrong with each other. Unknown

A playboy is a man who wines them and dines them before he reclines them. Unknown

A playboy is a man who believes in life, liberty, and the happiness of pursuit. Unknown

A smile is a pleasant expression that always adds to a person's face value. Unknown

Soft soap is what a woman uses to make a man slip into her arms. Unknown

A sophisticate is a girl who knows how to refuse an invitation to make love without being deprived of it. Unknown

He was awake a long time before he remembered that his heart was broken. Ernest Hemingway

Quotes on Sex, Love & Marriage

The smiles of a pretty woman are the tears of the purse. Italian Proverb

Anybody who believes that the way to a man's heart is through his stomach flunked geography. Robert Byrne

A spinster is one who said no once too often. Unknown

Jealousy is the injured lover's hell. Milton

If the world seems cold, kindle a fire to warm it. Fortune Cookie Wisdom

Life is a flower of which love is the honey. Victor Hugo

It is astonishing how little one feels poverty when one loves. Bulwer

Love is the most terrible, and also the most generous of the passions; it is the only one that includes in its dreams the happiness of someone else. J.A. Karr

Nobody is as sophisticated as a boy of nineteen who is just recovering from a baby-grand passion. Helen Rowland

A romance is 1 percent sense and 99 percent sensation. Unknown

A rake is a hit-an-run lover. Unknown

Quotes on Sex, Love & Marriage

A pushover is the only woman who goes out of a man's life without slamming the door. Unknown

Be to her virtues very kind, be to her faults a little blind. Matthew Prior

The romance is the period when a box of candy mean friendship, a bunch of flowers means love, and a diamond means business. Unknown

Romance is the feeling that makes a young man want to call a girl by his last name. Unknown

A man reserves his greatest and deepest love not for the woman in whose company he finds himself electrified and enkindled, but for that one in whose company he may feel tenderly drowsy. George Jean Nathan

There is no such thing as romance in our day, women have become too brilliant. Oscar Wilde

A suitor is a young man who rises early with the sun but stays up late with the daughter. Unknown

A summer resort is a vacation spot where girls go to look for husbands, and husbands go to look for girls. Unknown

Surprise is something unexpected, like finding a good-looker on a blind date. Unknown

Quotes on Sex, Love & Marriage

Walk with a good heart and you will run with success. Fortune Cookie Wisdom

A suitor is a young man who asks for the daughter's hand and sometimes gets the father's foot. Unknown

When a young man complains that a young lady has no heart, it is pretty certain that she has his. George Prentice

Love must be learned, and learned again and again; there is no end to it. Hate needs no instruction, but waits only to be provoked. Katherine Anne Porter

It is a beautiful necessity of our nature to love something. Jerrold

I am not one of those who do not believe in love at first sight, but I believe in taking a second look. H. Vincent

It is better to have loved and lost, than not to love at all. Tennyson

The great happiness of life is the conviction that we are loved, loved for ourselves, or rather loved in spite of ourselves. Victor Hugo

Hope is love's happiness, but not its life. L.E. Landon

Quotes on Sex, Love & Marriage

Blessed is the influence of one true, loving human soul on another. George Eliot

Nostalgia is the triumph of sentiment over memory. Unknown

Perfume is a feminine lure devised to take a young man's mind off sports. Unknown

Puberty is the period when a girl loses her faith in fairy tales and begins to believe in love. Unknown

Single is what a philanderer means when he tells a woman he loves her just the way she is. Unknown

Nostalgia is dreaming of the days and dames gone by.
Unknown

A singles club is a club whose members of both sexes are eager to double up. Unknown

Shyness is the lack of self-confidence that makes a marriageable young man hope the right girl will pick him out.
Unknown

A star is an actress to whom marriage is seldom a lifelong trip on the sea of matrimony, but rather a series of short cruises.
Unknown

Love is an egotism of two. La Salle

Quotes on Sex, Love & Marriage

A woman is never too old to be touched by the faithfulness of an old lover. Evelyn Schuyler Schaeffer

In the eyes of a lover, pockmarks are dimples. Japanese Proverb

Love sought is good, but given unsought is better. Shakespeare

I never could explain why I loved anybody, or anything. Walt Whitman

A starlet is a young movie actress who has been married only once. Unknown

Nostalgia is memory with the pain and tears removed. Unknown

A philanderer is a man who is first troubled by women who cannot forget him, and later by women who cannot remember him. Unknown

Love is the pleasure you cannot measure. Unknown

Love is a game that usually ends in a tie . Unknown

Love is a path that is only wide enough for two. Unknown

Love is the misunderstanding between a man and a woman. Unknown

Quotes on Sex, Love & Marriage

Love is the only fire against which there is no insurance.
Unknown

Being infatuated is being completely carried away by love for a woman without any faults. Unknown

Infatuation is the mystery of how a miss can fool a mister.
Unknown

Infatuation is an intense feeling when nothing so unmans a man as a woman. Unknown

Infatuation is the only kind of fire that is never covered by insurance or assurances of any kind. Unknown

Infatuation is a malady common among young people who never seek a second opinion. Unknown

Infatuation is the state when a man is out of his mind because there's a woman in it. Unknown

Infatuation is a condition where a young man loses his head and heart at the same time. Unknown

Infatuation is an intense feeling when half the fun of being in love is the worry of it. Unknown

Sex lies at the root of life, and we can never learn to reverence life until we know how to understand sex. Havelock Ellis

Quotes on Sex, Love & Marriage

Infatuation is the state of mind that makes a young man think nothing is good enough for a girl - except himself. Unknown

Infatuation is an emotional state when a man first makes a fool of himself and lets the girl finish the job. Unknown

Infatuation is the emotional state when the wilder a man is about a woman, the easier it is for her to tame him. Unknown

Infatuation is the short period when a girl sweeps a man off his feet, followed by a long period when he has her on his hands. Unknown

Infatuation is what makes a young man go about with a vacant look when a girl is constantly occupying his mind. Unknown

Infatuation is a mad passion that makes a man buy a girl something she doesn't need at a price he can't afford. Unknown

Love is a season pass on the shuttle between heaven and hell. Unknown

Love is one damn thing after another, or two damn things after each other. Unknown

Love is a romantic feeling that sharpens all the senses except common sense . Unknown

Quotes on Sex, Love & Marriage

Maybe in order to understand sex fully/one has to risk being destroyed by it. Sharon Olds

Love is a feeling that flatters your ego while it flattens your wallet. Unknown

Love is a condition of the mind when the mind is out of condition. Unknown

A love letter is the only letter worth keeping, especially if it is one that should never have been written. Unknown

A lovelorn man often turns to drink to forget the woman who is driving him to drink. Unknown

Lovelorn is the girl who cannot put a man out of her mind after he has put her out of his life. Unknown

The best way to makeup is to kiss your sweetheart and say you're sorry. Unknown

We tend to think of the erotic as an easy, tantalizing sexual arousal. I speak of the erotic as the deepest life force, a force which moves us toward living in a fundamental way. Audre Lorde

Love is an emotion that makes marriage possible before habit makes it endurable. Unknown

Quotes on Sex, Love & Marriage

A confirmed bachelor is an amorous who is free to choose, and chooses to be free. Unknown

A coed is a college student who sometimes loves to learn but more often learns to love. Unknown

Romance is the only sport in which the animal that gets caught has to buy the license. Unknown

Coeducation is a system under which some college girls pursue learning, while most learn pursuing. Unknown

Love is a fire. But whether it is going to warm your heart or burn down your house, you can never tell. Unknown

A smart girl is one who can refuse a kiss without being deprived of it. Unknown

A bachelor is one who can have a girl on his knees without having her on his hands. Unknown

Some college girls spend as much time pursuing a bachelor as a bachelor's degree. Unknown

A confirmed bachelor is a philander who has taken out many a girl, but has never been taken in. Unknown

A confirmed bachelor is a professional bachelor who plays the game of love without losing his amateur status. Unknown

Quotes on Sex, Love & Marriage

Love is a condition that brings a flutter to the heart and a flatter to the tongue. Unknown

Love is a romantic attachment that creates illusions without providing for their future upkeep. Unknown

Love is the only game in which the amateur has a better chance than the professional. Unknown

A philanderer likes to go out with girls who stay up till the oui hours of the morning. Unknown

Sensuality is the fuel of love that turns one into the fool of love. Unknown

Spring is when a young man's fancy lightly turns to something fancy. Unknown

Spring is that wonderful time of year when the trees begin to dress and women begin to do the opposite. Unknown

A philanderer is a womanizer whose experience in the art of love had taught him that it is more important to know when than how. Unknown

A pickup is a girl who defies the law of gravity: It is easier to pick her up than to drop her. Unknown

Platonic love is the period between the first meeting and the first kiss. Unknown

Quotes on Sex, Love & Marriage

The heart has its reasons which reason does not understand.
Blaise Pascal

Courtship consists in a number of quiet attentions, not so pointed as to alarm, nor so vague as not to be understood.
Laurence Sterne

The human heart, at whatever age, opens only to the heart that opens in return. Maria Edgeworth

In love, as in war, a fortress that parleys is half taken.
Margaret of Valois

In the race for love, I was scratched. Joan Davis

Why is it so difficult to love wisely, so easy to love too well?
Mary E. Braddon

The loveliest of faces are to be seen by moonlight, when one sees half with the eye and half with the fancy. Persian Proverb

By the time you swear you're his, shivering and sighing, and he vows his passion is infinite, undying - lady, make a note of this: one of you is lying. Dorothy Parker

The wrinkles of the heart are more indelible than those of the brow. Deluzy

Love is the lodestone of love. Mrs. Osgood

Quotes on Sex, Love & Marriage

Like the measles, love is most dangerous when it comes late in life. Lord Byron

To be in love is merely to be in a perpetual state of anesthesia. H.L. Mencken

Love concedes in a moment what we can hardly attain by effort after years of toil. Goethe

The advantage of emotions is that they lead us astray. Oscar Wilde

A romantic is the girl who sprains her imagination and thinks she has a broken heart. Unknown

A shrew is a woman who, because she wears the pants, eventually finds some other woman wearing the fur coat. Unknown

Soft soap is what a girls uses to get a ring off her finger or to get one on. Unknown

Sophistication is sending your girlfriend nineteen roses on her twenty-fifth birthday. Unknown

A romantic is the girl who dreams about being swept off her feet by a man she has eating out of her hand. Unknown

A smile is the curve that usually sets things straight. Unknown

Quotes on Sex, Love & Marriage

A romantic is an unrealistic young woman who, once she has given you her heart, will give you the rest of her body. Unknown

Friendship is like earthenware, once broken it can be mended; love is like a mirror, once broken, that ends it. Josh Billings

Love is a game that often begins with courting days and often ends with days in court. Unknown

Love is the only thing that enables a woman to look up to a man shorter than she is. Unknown

Love is a feeling that often begins with how a girl looks, and sometimes ends with how she cooks. Unknown

Love is an unbalanced state of mind when two people think as much of each other as they think of themselves. Unknown

Love is a form of insanity that makes a girl marry her boss and work for him the rest of her life without salary. Unknown

A lover's quarrel is a number of damns obstructing the course of love. Unknown

Marriage is an interlude between romances. Unknown

A lover is one who never leaves a girl in the dark. Unknown

Quotes on Sex, Love & Marriage

Opportunism is picking up a girl on another fellow's whistle.
Unknown

Perfume is another case where art improves on nature.
Unknown

Love is the greatest refreshment in life. Pablo Picasso

You've got to love what's loveable, and hate what's hateable. It takes brains to see the difference. Robert Frost

Love doesn't make the world go 'round. Love is what makes the ride worthwhile. Franklin P. Jones

Perfume is a pretty gift that costs a man a pretty cent.
Unknown

Optimism is the state of mind that believes matrimony will be cheaper than the courtship. Unknown

A lover is one who never objects to the price, which is why all the world loves a lover. Unknown

Love is a game in which the wisest of men are foolish about women, but the most foolish of women are wise about men.
Unknown

Love is a state of mind that begins when you think life couldn't be any better, and ends when you think it couldn't be any worse. Unknown

Quotes on Sex, Love & Marriage

A love affair is an attachment that often leads to marriage and almost as often to divorce. Unknown

A love affair is a liaison that any amateur can start but only a professional knows how to break off. Unknown

Jealousy is something that starts with the arrival of a rival. Unknown

Jealousy is a violent emotion that turns a kittenish woman into a cat. Unknown

Jealousy is what makes a woman hate the woman who gets the man she discarded. Unknown

Jealousy is the imagination that makes up in suspicion what it lacks in knowledge. Unknown

Jealousy is an emotion that makes you suffer delusions because you jumped to conclusions. Unknown

A kiss is a contraction of the mouth due to the enlargement of the heart. Unknown

A laugh is a smile that has burst. Unknown

Loneliness is one of the few things worse than a quarrel. Unknown

Quotes on Sex, Love & Marriage

A kiss is something you cannot give without taking, and cannot take without giving. Unknown

Jealousy is the state of mind that forces a woman to ask more questions but believe fewer answers. Unknown

Jealousy is the spirit that makes a woman look her best, especially when she's out to do her worst. Unknown

A love affair is when two people who never tire of being together, because they are always talking about themselves. Unknown

The pleasure of love lies in loving, and our own sensations make us happier than those we inspire. LaRochefoucauld

What is a romantic? One who, when life is too banal or too lazy to manufacture tragedy for him, creates it artificially, thus getting himself into the hot water he himself has boiled. Clifton Fadiman

Newness is to love what their bloom is to fruits; it creates a lustre which is easily lost and which never returns. LaRochefoucauld

A love affair is an emotional experience that you never forget because it is something you always learn by heart. Unknown

Quotes on Sex, Love & Marriage

A love affair is an amorous relationship where a man is sometimes attracted to a girl by her mind, but more often by what she doesn't mind. Unknown

A drive-in theater is a place not for people who love to go to the movies, but for people who go to the movies to love. Unknown

A flatterer is a woman who has found a much easier way to a man's heart than through his stomach. Unknown

A flirt is the woman whose eyes meet yours before she meets you. Unknown

A gold digger is the type of woman who is never torn between love and booty. Unknown

The golf course is the most likely place for a woman to find a husband. Unknown

A hairdo is what a girl spends a lot of care and money on in the hopes that some man will mess it up. Unknown

Heaven grant us patience with a man in love. Rudyard Kipling

A love song is just a caress set to music. Sigmund Romberg

Love is said to be blind but I know some fellows who can see twice as much in their sweethearts as I do. Josh Billings

Quotes on Sex, Love & Marriage

One is certain of nothing but the truth of one's emotions. E.M. Forster

A part of kindness consists in loving people more than they deserve. Joseph Joubert

A good-for-nothing is a person who, no matter how worthless he is, can always find a woman and a dog that will love him. Unknown

Dating is the period when it's never amiss to kiss a miss. Unknown

Dating is a romantic period when one's income influences its outcome. Unknown

Dating is a game during which a girl pursues a cagey man until she cages him. Unknown

Courtship is the stage in a woman's life when her instinct tells her whether a man needs inducement or discouragement. Unknown

The divorcee is the woman who feels like a new man. Unknown

A flatterer is one who turns a woman's head by telling her she has a beautiful profile. Unknown

Quotes on Sex, Love & Marriage

A flatterer is a person whose overpraise makes others feel good because they know they deserve it. Unknown

Glamour is the alluring charm that surrounds a woman, especially when there are a few drinks in a man. Unknown

A gold digger is the perfect match for the man who has money to burn. Unknown

A glamour girl is a one who is very easy on the eyes, but hard on the wallet. Unknown

Dating is a romantic time when a girl begins to call you by your first name because it's your last name she's after.
Unknown

There's no fool like an old fool, you can't beat experience.
Jacob M. Braude

A platonic friendship is an unhealthy lie. John Oliver Hobbes

Those sweetly smiling angels with pensive looks, innocent faces, and cash-boxes for hearts. Honore De Balzac

Few people, when they love no longer, feel shame for having loved. LaRochefoucauld

Self-interest blinds some people and sharpens the eyesight of others. LaRochefoucauld

Quotes on Sex, Love & Marriage

Friendship may, and often does, grow into love; but love never subsides into friendship. Lord Byron

Here's to woman! Would that we could fall into her arms without falling into her hands. Ambrose Bierce

An advantage of having a hard heart is that it will take a lot to break it. W. Burton Baldry

The surest way to hit a woman's heart is to take aim kneeling. Douglas Jerrold

Dating is the period during which the girl decides whether or not she can do any better. Unknown

Love is a grave mental illness. Plato

Dating is a game where the girl who puts all her cards on the table, ends up playing solitaire. Unknown

A crush is a sever case of he-fever, common among teenage girls. Unknown

A crush is a foolish state of mind that has nothing to do with the mind. Unknown

The dance floor is where some women love to dance and others dance to love. Unknown

Quotes on Sex, Love & Marriage

A flirt is a woman who uses her eyes to attract a husband, but never her own. Unknown

A flirt is a girl who spends her time making temporary male friends, but permanent female enemies. Unknown

A dancing partner is a man who, if he can't dance, can at least hold you while you dance. Unknown

A crush is the love that begins at first sight and ends with a second look. Unknown

She would have made a splendid wife, for crying only made her eyes more bright and tender. O. Henry

There are two sorts of faithfulness in love: one is based on forever finding new things to love in the loved one; the other is based on our pride in being faithful. LaRochefoucauld

To say you can love one person all your life is just like saying that one candle will continue burning as long as you live. Leo Tolstoy

Love is the wine of existence. Henry Ward Beecher

Never a lip is curved with pain that can't be kissed into smiles again. Bret Harte

Love, like fire, must constantly leap and dart; when it can neither hope nor fear, it dies. LaRochefoucauld

Quotes on Sex, Love & Marriage

Love lasteth as long as the money endureth. William Caxton

Women in love are less ashamed than men. They have less to be ashamed of. Ambrose Bierce

Love is a conflict between reflexes and reflections. Magnus Hirschfeld

Happiness isn't an outside job, it's an inside job. Fortune Cookie Wisdom

Tears are the noble language of the eye. Robert Herrick

A crush is the first foolish love affair that a woman cherishes, and a man forgets. Unknown

A crush is a romantic state that begins when a girl finds her dream man, and ends when she wakes up. Unknown

Gold digger: a human gimme pig. Unknown

Love is like a well; all right to taste of but bad to fall into. Unknown

If there is anything better than to be loved, it is loving. Unknown

Quotes on Sex, Love & Marriage

No woman ever hates a man for being in love with her, but many a woman hates a man for being a friend to her. Alexander Pope

Women often falsely imagine they are in love. the excitement of an intrigue, the emotions aroused by sex, the instinctive enjoyment of being wooed and the difficulties of saying no, all give them an illusion of passion where nothing exists beyond coquetry. LaRochefoucauld

A relationship is what happens between two people who are waiting for something better to come along. Unknown

When people have fallen out of love, they find a sore problem to break off. LaRochefoucauld

The greatest miracle of love is that it stamps out coquetry. LaRochefoucauld

The quickest way to go broke is to start loving beyond your means. Unknown

Most of these love triangles are wrecktangles. Unknown

Fox: a wolf that sends flowers. Unknown

Gold digger: a girl who breaks dates by going out with them. Unknown

Quotes on Sex, Love & Marriage

Happiness is like a kiss - in order to get any good out of it you have to give it to somebody else. Unknown

A corkscrew is the turning point in many a girl's life. Unknown

Courtship is a contest during which a couple is often on the verge of breaking up before she finally breaks him down. Unknown

We are equally hard to satisfy when we are passionately in love and when we have almost ceased to care. LaRochefoucauld

A gentleman in love may behave like a madman but not like a dunce. LaRochefoucauld

We can love those we hate more easily that those who love us more than we want them to. LaRochefoucauld

In love deception almost always exceeds distrust. LaRochefoucauld

The suffering we go through to keep from loving is often worse than the hardships endured for love. LaRochefoucauld

Jealousy is always born with love, but does not always die with it. LaRochefoucauld

The corkscrew is the best thing with which to open a conversation. Unknown

Quotes on Sex, Love & Marriage

Courtship is a ship that has two mates and no captain.
Unknown

Courtship is the romantic time when a young man is bound to love beyond his means. Unknown

A courtship to the romantic girl is moonlight and roses; to the realistic man, sunlight and ruses. Unknown

Courtship is an exciting time when late hours are bad for one but good for two. Unknown

Courtship is the short period of long kisses followed by a long period of short kisses. Unknown

In friendship, as in love, we are often happier not knowing things than knowing them. LaRochefoucauld

Young women who would not be talked of as flirts and old men who would not be taken for fools should never speak of love as anything that personally concerns them. LaRochefoucauld

It is almost always the fault of the one in love not to realize that the other one no longer is. LaRochefoucauld

All the passions force us to make mistakes, but love causes the most ridiculous ones. LaRochefoucauld

Quotes on Sex, Love & Marriage

There are all kinds of cures for love, but none that are infallible. LaRochefoucauld

Of all violent passions, love suits women least badly. LaRochefoucauld

There are people so self-centered that when they are in love they manage to dwell on their passion without a thought of the person who inspires it. LaRochefoucauld

The influence that those we love have over us almost always exceeds our influence over ourselves. LaRochefoucauld

Lovers only notice their mistresses' faults when their mistresses' fascination has ended. LaRochefoucauld

Prudence and love are ill-mated: for always as love increases, prudence declines. LaRochefoucauld

Courtship is a mating game that began ages ago with clubs and is now played with diamonds. Unknown

Courtship is a contest where a little flattery now and then makes husbands out of single men. Unknown

Courtship is a subterfuge where the wiles of women are stronger than the wills of men. Unknown

A kiss is a rosy dot placed on the 'i' in loving. Unknown

Quotes on Sex, Love & Marriage

A bachelor is a man who never Mrs. anybody. Unknown

Chivalry: a man's inclination to defend a woman against every man but himself. Unknown

Charm: the ability to make someone else think that both of you are pretty wonderful. Unknown

Gold digger: a young woman who likes to go buy buy. Unknown

Falling in love is easier than falling out of it. LaRochefoucauld

When we love too much, we are seldom aware of being loved no longer. LaRochefoucauld

A sure way to arouse love is to love very little yourself. LaRochefoucauld

The frankness that lovers and mistresses insist in, the understanding between them that they be told when they are loved no longer, is much less a wish to be told so, than a kind of guarantee that they are loved until told otherwise. LaRochefoucauld

Champagne: a beverage that makes you see double and feel single. Unknown

Love is an intoxication of the nervous system. Unknown

Quotes on Sex, Love & Marriage

Courtship is the period when there's no fool like an old fool who tries to act like a young fool. Unknown

Courtship is an amorous deception when a girl doesn't say all she means, and a man doesn't mean all he says. Unknown

One must have loved a woman of genius in order to comprehend what happiness there is in loving a fool. Talleyrand

Quotes on Sex, Love & Marriage

Quotes on Marriage & Weddings

I have a dog that growls, a parrot that swears, a stove that smokes, and a cat that stays out all night. Why do I need a husband? Unknown

The honeymoon's over when the groom stops praising his wife's clothes and starts pricing them. Unknown

A wedding ring is a circle around a woman's finger, but a noose around a man's neck. Unknown

When he finally proposed she was so excited she fell out of bed. Unknown

It's pretty hard to keep up with the Joneses, especially when they are newlyweds. Unknown

My husband doesn't munch words! Mary Carter

I'd like to get married because I like the idea of a man being required by law to sleep with me every night. Carrie Snow

The woman cries before the wedding; the man afterward. Polish Proverb

A wedding ring is a tourniquet on the finger that stops your circulation. Unknown

Quotes on Sex, Love & Marriage

When the two teenagers were turned down by the Marriage License Bureau, they asked, "Could you maybe give us a learner's permit?" Unknown

A wedding is a service where woman accepts man for the sake of marriage, and man accepts marriage for the sake of woman. Unknown

The best years of a man's life is just before he stumbles and Mrs. Unknown

The most shocked women in the world are those who get married because they got tired of working. Unknown

My toughest fight was with my first wife. Muhammad Ali

Marriage is a bargain, and someone has to get the worst of a bargain. Helen Rowland

Almost all married people fight, although many are ashamed to admit it. Actually a marriage in which no quarreling at all takes place may well be one that is dead or dying from emotional undernourishment. If you care, you probably fight. Flora Davis

He who marries might be sorry. He who does not will be sorry. Czechoslovakian Proverb

When a girl proposes to a man she isn't any more comfortable about it than a man is when he does. Unknown

Quotes on Sex, Love & Marriage

A wedding ceremony is where a man takes his wife for better or worse, and then begins to take her for granted. Unknown

Wedding cake is the only cake which, once eaten, can give you indigestion for the rest of your life. Unknown

A wedding dress is what a bride formerly saved for her daughter but now saves for her next wedding. Unknown

The wedding march is a beautiful piece of music that's a little too slow to hum while washing the dishes. Unknown

A wedding ring is what a man gives his girl when he cannot afford to go steady with her any longer. Unknown

Wedlock is the disillusion of the man who agreed to marriage before finding out that marriage does not agree with him. Unknown

A wedding is a ceremony where the bride looks stunning and the groom looks stunned. Unknown

A proposal is a sentence ending with a proposition. Unknown

A proposal is an offer of marriage when even the man of few words talks to much. Unknown

Quotes on Sex, Love & Marriage

After a few years of marriage, a man can look right at a woman without seeing her - and a woman can see right through a man without looking at him. Helen Rowland

The honeymoon is the period during which the bride trusts the bridegroom's word of honor. Unknown

You never hear of a man marrying a woman to reform her. Unknown

Optimism is the state of mind which believes matrimony will be cheaper than the engagement. Unknown

A stenographer is a girl who learns to type on your time while she waiting for a chance to get married. Unknown

To his bride said the lynx-eyed detective,
"Can it be that my eyesight's defective?
   Has your east tit the least bit
   The best of the west tit?
Or is it a trick of perspective?" Unknown

Many a man owes his success to his first wife, and his second wife to his success. Jim Backus

Some men think that being married to a woman means merely seeing her in the mornings instead of the evenings. Helen Rowland

Quotes on Sex, Love & Marriage

Marry for money, my little sonny, a rich man's joke is always funny. Hebrew Proverb

A proposal is an offer of marriage when a young man makes the best speech he'll ever regret. Unknown

Remarriage is the part of the sea of matrimony where the second mate seldom becomes the captain. Unknown

A romantic is the kind of girl who expects too much of marriage, and who gets just what she expects - too much of marriage. Unknown

Every woman who hasn't any money is a matrimonial adventurer. Bernard Shaw

A wife is not to be chosen by the eye only. Choose a wife rather by your ear than your eye. Thomas Fuller

A man in love is incomplete until he has married. Then he's finished. Zsa Zsa Gabor

When you see what some girls marry you realize how they must hate to work for a living. Helen Rowland

Marriage is the only evil that men pray for. Arab Proverb

Why does a woman work ten years to change a man's habits and then complain that he's not the man she married. Barbara Streisand

Quotes on Sex, Love & Marriage

A proposal is an offer of marriage where the girl listens faster than the man can talk. Unknown

Remarriage is the proof that one man's mate is another man's poison. Unknown

The modern debutante no longer comes out, she's carried out. Gregory Nunn

Wives are liars by law. John Galsworthy

Any intelligent woman who reads the marriage contract, and then goes into it, deserves all the consequences. Isadora Duncan

It isn't tying himself to one woman that a man dreads when he thinks of marrying; it's separating himself from all the others. Helen Rowland

Wives and watermelons are picked by chance. Greek Proverb

Remarriage is a connubial retake when a man gets a new leash on life. Unknown

A proposal is an offer of marriage during which the man is nervous and the girl stops being nervous. Unknown

A wedding is the ritual marking the time when a woman stops dating and starts intimidating. Unknown

Quotes on Sex, Love & Marriage

The happiest man at a wedding is the bridegroom's father-in-law. Unknown

In the wedding ceremony the wife loses her name and the husband loses his freedom. Unknown

A wedding is a conjugal ceremony that is unlucky to postpone, unless you keep on doing it. Unknown

The wedding is the dividing line between the romanticism of courtship and the realism of marriage. Unknown

A wedding is a service that proves that a man with will power is no match for a woman with wile power. Unknown

Remarriage is the event after a marital mess when a divorcee makes a clean sweep with a new groom. Unknown

A wedding is a service that changes the soft-spoken bride of today into the oftspoken wife of tomorrow. Unknown

The wages of sin is alimony. Carolyn Wells

An archaeologist is the best husband any woman can have: the older she gets, the more interested he is in her. Agatha Christie

There were two bothers who were smart and a third who got married. Polish Proverb

Quotes on Sex, Love & Marriage

It is always incomprehensible to a man that a woman should ever refuse an offer of marriage. Jane Austin

A wedding is where a women promises to share a man's lot, unaware that it may be a lot of trouble. Unknown

A wedding is the joining together that is always happy, followed by the living together that causes all the trouble. Unknown

A wedding is a ceremony where a girl sometimes marries a man because he is rich or handsome, but more often because he asked her. Unknown

The more a man knows, and the father he travels, the more likely he is to marry a country girl afterwards. Bernard Shaw

For talk six times with the same single lady, and you may get the wedding dress ready. Lord Byron

Marriage is the miracle that transforms a kiss from a pleasure into a duty. Helen Rowland

It is matrimonial suicide to be jealous when you have a really good reason. Clare Boothe Luce

He who marries for money earns it. Hebrew Proverb

Quotes on Sex, Love & Marriage

Marriage is a lottery in which if you lose you can't tear up the ticket. Helen Rowland

Keep in mind that the home is where the heart is. Fortune Cookie Wisdom

Nobody knows why men marry, so its best to make the most of any chance you happen to get. Mary L. Pendered

Any woman will marry any man that bothers her enough. Henry Wallace Phillips

To get married is to tie a knot with the tongue that you cannot undue with your teeth. E.M. Wright

A wedding is the bridal day that turns the girl that is dear to your heart into a woman who is dear to your purse. Unknown

A wedding is a ritual where the father gives up his daughter with reluctance, and a mother gives her up with relief. Unknown

A womanizer is a playboy who will take a pretty girl anywhere she wants to go except to the altar. Unknown

On the whole, I haven't found men unduly loath to say, " I love you." The real trick is to get them to say, " Will you marry me." Ilka Chase

Quotes on Sex, Love & Marriage

I knew her when she didn't know where her next husband was coming from. Anne Baxter

The most popular labor-saving device today is still a husband with money. Joey Adams

Love comes after the wedding. Lapp Proverb

Husband: what is left of the lover after the nerve has been extracted. Helen Rowland

A wedding is much ado about ' I do. ' Unknown

A wedding is a funeral where you smell your own flowers. Unknown

A wedding is a ceremony at which a man loses control of himself. Unknown

A son-in-law is what every girl hopes her mother will have. Unknown

A star is an actor who marries for love and keeps on marrying until he gets it. Unknown

A starlet is a junior star whose first movie usually lasts longer than her first marriage. Unknown

A girl is usually straight until she becomes bent on matrimony. Unknown

Quotes on Sex, Love & Marriage

Tomorrow is the best day to get married. Unknown

A trousseau is a form of gift wrapping for the bride. Unknown

Marriage is the sunset of love. French Proverb

A starlet is a young movie star who will probably make a glamorous wife for half a dozen men. Unknown

God help the man who won't marry until he finds a perfect woman, and God help him still more if he finds her. Ben Tillett

Nobody works as hard for his money as the man who marries it. Kin Hubbard

A second marriage is the triumph of hope over experience. Samuel Johnson

Mistakes show us what we need to learn. Fortune Cookie Wisdom

Man's biggest mistake is to believe that he's working for someone else. Fortune Cookie Wisdom

Life is about making some things happen, not waiting for something to happen. Fortune Cookie Wisdom

Quotes on Sex, Love & Marriage

In the divorce process, time can be just as heavy a ball and chain as the marriage was. Robert H. Williams

A light wife doth make a heavy husband. Shakespeare

I chose my wife, as she did her wedding gown, for qualities that would wear well. Goldsmith

You will share great news with all the people you love. Fortune Cookie Wisdom

Married in haste, we repent at leisure. Congreve

Of all the actions of a man' life, his marriage does least concern other people, yet of all actions of our life, 'tis most meddled with by other people. Seldon

If you wish to ruin yourself, marry a rich wife. Michelet

Marriage with a good woman is a harbor in the tempest of life; with a bad woman, it is a tempest in the harbor. J.P. Senn

Men marry to make an end; women to make a beginning. A. Dupuy

Wedlock's like wine, not properly judged of till the second glass. Jerrold

Hanging and wiving go by destiny. Shakespeare

Quotes on Sex, Love & Marriage

A mutual and satisfied sexual act is of great benefit to the average woman, the magnetism of it is health giving. When it is not desired on the part of the woman and she has no response, it should not take place. This is an act of prostitution and is degrading to the woman's finer sensibility, all the marriage certificates on earth to the contrary notwithstanding. Margaret Sanger

There is more of good nature than of good sense at the bottom of most marriages. Thoreau

A starlet is a young actress who is so thrilled with her first marriage, she can hardly wait for the next. Unknown

A wedding is the ceremony in which a woman acquires another mind of her own. Unknown

When a man and woman are married their romance ceases and their history commences. Rochebrune

A wedding is a celebration where the bride isn't really happy, just triumphant. Unknown

A friend married is a friend lost. Henrik Ibsen

A shotgun wedding is a matter of wife or death. Unknown

Silver wedding is the anniversary on which a married man celebrates 25 years of work under the same boss. Unknown

Quotes on Sex, Love & Marriage

It's no lack to lack a wife. English Proverb

Silence is another thing that marriage helps bring out in a man. Unknown

A secretary is an employee who, when she marries her boss, gets off his lap and into his hair. Unknown

Bigamy is one way of avoiding the painful publicity of divorce and the expense of alimony. Oliver Herford

A wedding is the ritual at which a man becomes a captive audience for his wife. Unknown

Marriage is a field in which amateurs have the best chance of success. Unknown

Marriage is the cure for mental cases where people are crazy about each other. Unknown

Marriage is an unhappy result of asking a foolish question and getting a foolish answer. Unknown

An ideal husband is the man who never quarrels, never gambles - and never marries. Unknown

Infatuation is an intense passion that makes a man marry in haste and later pay alimony at leisure. Unknown

Quotes on Sex, Love & Marriage

Love is a tender feeling that should be behind every wedding, bit not too far behind. Unknown

A lovelorn girl is one who doesn't want to marry the man she can be happy with, but pines for the man she cannot be happy without. Unknown

A lover is a man who, if crossed in love, remains a bachelor, but if double-crossed, becomes a husband. Unknown

M is the letter beginning marriage and ending freedom. Unknown

A love affair is a romantic episode when a girl's hardest job is to convince a man that his intentions are serious. Unknown

Love is a driving force that makes a girl marry a man in spite of her parent's urging. Unknown

Marriage is the period between the I do's of the wedding and the adieus of the divorce. Unknown

Marriage is a beautiful custom in which two people share all the troubles their marriage created. Unknown

Marriage is a partnership that begins with a small payment to a minister and often ends with a large payment to a lawyer. Unknown

Quotes on Sex, Love & Marriage

Marriage is a duet for two voices that are not always in harmony. Unknown

Marriage is the first of all unions to go in for on-the-job training. Unknown

Marriage is an institution that gives a man double the duties and half the rights. Unknown

When singleness is bliss, it's folly to be wives. Bill Counselman

An optimist is one who believes marriage is a gamble. Laurence J. Peter

All work and no play makes Jack a dull boy - and Jill a wealthy widow. Evan Esar

Marriage! Nothing else demands so much from a man! Ibsen

Love in marriage should be the accomplishment of a beautiful dream, and not, as it too often is, the end. Karr

What no wife of a writer can ever understand is that a writer is working when he's staring out of the window. Burton Rascoe

I could do without your face, and without your neck, and your hands, and your limbs, and, to save myself the trouble of mentioning the points in detail, I could do without you altogether. Marcus Martial

Quotes on Sex, Love & Marriage

I like him and his wife. He is so ladylike, and she is such a perfect gentleman. Sidney Smith

A sound marriage is not based on complete frankness; it is based on sensible reticence. Morris Ernst

As bad as marrying the devil's daughter and living with the old folks. G.L. Apperson

Marriage is a mistake every man should make. George Jessel

Memory is what tells a man that his wife's birthday was yesterday. Mario Rocco

A wedding is a ceremony that altars a man's life, liberty and his pursuit of happiness. Unknown

Marriage is Heaven and Hell. German Proverb

In olden times sacrifices were made at the alter, a custom which still continues in marriage. Helen Rowland

Marriage is much more necessary to a man than a woman; for he is much less able to supply himself with domestic comforts. Samuel Johnson

Keep your eyes wide open before marriage and half-shut afterwards. Benjamin Franklin

Quotes on Sex, Love & Marriage

Marriage begins when women stop dating and start intimidating. Unknown

A man has no business to marry a woman who can't make him miserable; it means that she can't make him happy. Unknown

Many a girl who can't stand a man's ways marries him for his means. Unknown

A man who gives in when he is wrong is wise. A man who gives in when he is right is married. Unknown

To marry a woman for her beauty is like buying a house for its paint. Unknown

When a girl marries, she exchanges the attentions of many men for the inattention of one. Helen Rowland

Married couples who love each other, tell each other a thousand things without talking. Chinese Proverb

Some men feel that the only thing they owe the woman who marries them is a grudge. Helen Rowland

Optimism is the man who believes the woman he is about to marry is better than the one he has divorced. Unknown

Procrastination is the proof that all things come to him who waits, including an invitation to his girlfriend's wedding. Unknown

Quotes on Sex, Love & Marriage

Progress is the development of society from two-way streets and one-way marriages to one-way streets and two-way marriages. Unknown

Husbands are like fires. They go out when unattended. Zsa Zsa Gabor

Marrying a man is like buying something you've been admiring for a long time in a shop window. You may love it when you get it home, but it doesn't always go with everything else in the house. Jean Kerr

Wedlock- the deep, deep peace of the double bed after the hurly-burly of the chaise-lounge. Mrs. Patrick Campbell

The wedding is the point at which a man stops toasting a woman and begins roasting her. Helen Rowland

It was so cold the other day, I almost got married. Shelly Winters

To be merely marriageable, a girl had to have a fine large bottom or a fine large dowry. If she happened to have both, she was really sitting pretty. Stella Reichman

The most dangerous food a man can eat is wedding cake. American Proverb

Quotes on Sex, Love & Marriage

Polygamy is the practice of marriage where the wives fight each other instead of their husbands. Unknown

Waiting for a man to get ready to get married is like waiting for an egg to fry itself. Unknown

Don't marry for money, you can borrow it cheaper. Unknown

Did you hear about the media man who got married last week and traded reach for frequency. Unknown

A happy marriage is when they are both in love with him. Unknown

A good marriage would be between a blind woman and a deaf husband. Michel De Montaigne

Tragedy is a bride without a can opener. Unknown

If it were not for the presents, an elopement would be preferable. George Ade

One of the keys to happiness is a bad memory. Fortune Cookie Wisdom

The only good husbands stay bachelors; they're too considerate to get married. Finley Peter Dunne

Heiresses are never jilted. George Meredith

Quotes on Sex, Love & Marriage

A newlywed is the married man who sleeps like a baby until he gets one. Unknown

Maids want nothing but husbands, and when they have them, they want everything. William Shakespeare

A newlywed is a husband who still thinks reason can win over emotion in an argument with his wife. Unknown

Poetic justice is what happens when the woman who laughs up her sleeve marries the man who talks through his hat. Unknown

A newlywed is a man who soon learns not to hold his wife responsible today for what she said yesterday. Unknown

A newlywed is an illogical female who proclaims she married the perfect man, and then proceeds to remodel him. Unknown

Newlyweds are a married couple who need only one television set. Unknown

Matrimony is an entanglement that often starts with a simple wedding and ends with a complicated divorce. Unknown

Matrimony is the process of changing a girl who was hard to get into a woman who is hard to take. Unknown

Quotes on Sex, Love & Marriage

Matrimony is a union that begins with two people pulling together, and ends with one of them pulling out. Unknown

Marriage is a custom that was established because man did not feel complete until he had won back his missing rib. Unknown

Marriage is a legal union that formerly suffered from too much multiplying, but nowadays suffers from too much dividing. Unknown

A misogynist is a man who thinks every marriage license should have a divorce coupon attached. Unknown

Newlyweds are the young married couple whose plan for the future is mostly a credit plan. Unknown

Petting is a form of lovemaking that often ends in marriage, but more often by marriage. Unknown

Poetic justice is the marriage between the woman who says all men are alike and the man who says he understands women. Unknown

Newlyweds are a couple who are constantly being surprised because they think they understand each other. Unknown

Many a necklace becomes a noose. Paul Eldridge

'Tis better to have loved and lost, than to marry and be bossed. J.E. McCann

Quotes on Sex, Love & Marriage

One of the chief pleasures of middle age is looking at the picture of the girl you didn't marry. Dr. Laurence Peter

A husband is a sort of promissory note - a woman is tired of meeting him. Oscar Wilde

Long engagements give people the opportunity of finding out each other's character before marriage, which is never advisable. Oscar Wilde

Marriage is the hangover from the intoxication of love. Unknown

Marriage is the solution to a problem that creates many problems without solutions. Unknown

Marriage is a tie that transforms a girlfriend from a fascinating conversationalist into a wife who is better still. Unknown

Do not give up, the beginning is always the hardest. Fortune Cookie Wisdom

Marriage is an exchange that turns the wife who was his secretary before the wedding, into his treasurer afterward. Unknown

A marriage license is the only form of hunting license that is taken out after the hunt is over. Unknown

Quotes on Sex, Love & Marriage

A marriage proposal is a hitch pitch. Unknown

Marriage is a lifetime of housework that begins when a woman sweeps down the aisle. Unknown

Marriage is a venture that is often a failure, because so many inexperienced people go into it. Unknown

Marriage is an institution that turns the bride who doesn't know how to cook into the wife who certainly knows what's cooking. Unknown

Marriage is a wardrobe that begins with a wedding dress and ends with a divorce suit. Unknown

A honeymoon is the short period of doting between dating and debting. Unknown

The honeymoon is the period when a man treats a new wife like a new car. Unknown

Marriage is an institution in which a man constantly faces the music, beginning with, "Here Comes the Bride". Unknown

The man who marries to have someone to tell his troubles to soon has plenty to talk about. Unknown

Common sense could prevent most divorces - and most marriages. Unknown

Quotes on Sex, Love & Marriage

Bonds of matrimony: worthless unless the interest is kept up. Unknown

Insanity is grounds for divorce in some states, and grounds for marriage in them all. Unknown

Marriage is a romance in which the hero dies in the first chapter. Unknown

Marriage is a union between two people in which the man pays the dues. Unknown

Marriage is the process by which love ripens into vengeance. Unknown

He that climbs the tall tree has a right to the fruit. Fortune Cookie Wisdom

An optimist is one who marries his secretary thinking he'll continue to dictate to her. Unknown

Whether you wind up with a nest egg or a goose egg depends on the kind of chick you married. Wall Street Journal

Hollywood's favorite drink is marriage on the rocks. Unknown

Marriage is the way a man finds out what kind of husband his wife would have preferred. Unknown

Quotes on Sex, Love & Marriage

The honeymoon is the happy time when a woman isn't trying to reform her husband. Unknown

The honeymoon is the only time when a man doesn't think his wife talks too much. Unknown

The honeymoon is the only period when a wife cannot think of a better man she could have married. Unknown

The honeymoon is the time of greatest happiness during marriage, usually due to the absence of in-laws. Unknown

The days just prior to a marriage are like a snappy introduction to a tedious book. Wilson Mizner

A honeymoon is a good deal like a man laying off to take an expensive vacation, and coming back to a different job. Edgar Howe

Bigamy is having one wife too many, monogamy is the same. Oscar Wilde

To be wronged is nothing unless you continue to remember it. Fortune Cookie Wisdom

Alimony is a system which results when two people make a mistake and one of them continues to pay for it. Jimmy Lyons

Honeymoons are short periods of adjustment; marriages are long ones. Richard Sullivan

Quotes on Sex, Love & Marriage

What a holler would ensue, if people had to pay the minister as much to marry them as they have to pay a lawyer to get them a divorce. Claire Trevor

A man finds himself seven years older the day after his marriage. Francis Bacon

A working girl is one who quit her job to get married. E.J. Kiefer

When the blind lead the blind, they both fall into matrimony. George Farquhar

Matrimony: a woman's hair net tangled in a man's spectacles on top of the bedroom dresser. Don Herold

They stood before the altar and supplied the fire themselves in which their fat was fried. Ambrose Bierce

The honeymoon is over when he phones that he'll be late for supper, and she has already left a note that it's in the refrigerator. Bill Lawrence

Marriage is a good deal like taking a bath - not so hot once you get accustomed to it. Bill Lawrence

Marriage is the only known example of the happy meeting of the immovable object and the irresistible force. Ogden Nash

Quotes on Sex, Love & Marriage

A man's mother is his misfortune, but his wife is his own fault. Walter Bagehot

The honeymoon is the stage of marriage before he takes her off a pedestal and puts her on a budget. Unknown

The honeymoon is the period during which a man discovers his wife isn't an angel, so he quits posing as a saint. Unknown

So far no one has invented an intelligence test to equal matrimony. Unknown

The only comfort of my life is that I never yet had wife. Robert Herrick

By all means marry. If you get a good wife you will become happy-and if you get a bad one, you will become a philosopher. Socrates

A wife is a former sweetheart. H.L. Mencken

He who throws mud looses ground. Fortune Cookie Wisdom

Marriage is the most expensive way to get your laundry done. Charles James

Divorce is the sacrament of adultery. French Proverb

It's a funny thing that when a man hasn't anything on earth to worry about, he goes off and gets married. Robert Frost

Quotes on Sex, Love & Marriage

Marriage often unites for life two people who scarcely know each other. Honore de Balzac

A ring on the finger is worth two on the phone. Harold Thompson

Matrimony and bachelorhood are both of them at once equally wise and equally foolish. Samuel Butler

Call no man unhappy, until he is married. Socrates

The honeymoon is over when the dog brings your slippers and your wife barks at you. Unknown

Marriage is grounds for divorce. Unknown

Matrimony is like making a call. You go to adore, you ring a belle, you give your name to a maid...and then you are taken in. Unknown

A honeymoon is a vacation that ends when the bride stops dropping her eyes and starts raising her voice. Unknown

The honeymoon is the only period when husband and wife look at each other's faults with their eyes shut. Unknown

The honeymoon begins with a girl walking on air, and ends with her putting her foot down. Unknown

Quotes on Sex, Love & Marriage

Marriage is the mortgage a woman holds on a man's future.
Unknown

Marriage is a gamble where both players win, or both lose.
Unknown

A bride is the only thing that's not free when given away.
Unknown

A bride is another case where an amateur is preferable to a professional. Unknown

An economizer is the type of man many girls want to marry but few want to be engaged to. Unknown

Elopement is marrying on the spree of the moment. Unknown

Enthusiasm is contagious. Not having enthusiasm is also contagious. Fortune Cookie Wisdom

Elopement is the proof that love recognizes no law, not even a mother-in-law. Unknown

Elopement is a runaway marriage brought on when a man proposes and a mother-in-law opposes. Unknown

An elopement is a case of two people running away from home after their imaginations have run away with them. Unknown

Engagement is the overture to the wedding march. Unknown

Quotes on Sex, Love & Marriage

Engagement is when a girl in the race to the altar is on the last lap. Unknown

Engagement is the only period during which a girl is neither married nor single. Unknown

An engagement ring is the buy-product of love. Unknown

Engagement is a short period lacking in foresight, followed by a long period loaded with hindsight.

Engagement is the betrothal, when a couple spends half the time breaking up and the other half making up. Unknown

An engagement ring is a gift that is tied with heart-strings. Unknown

An engagement ring is the down payment on a wife-insurance policy. Unknown

It doesn't take guts to quit. Fortune Cookie Wisdom

An engagement ring is the proof that love is not blind, at least not stone blind. Unknown

An engagement ring is a ring that a young man gives his girl with all his heart and most of his savings. Unknown

Quotes on Sex, Love & Marriage

A bride is a girl who is usually given away by her father, and later by her girlfriends. Unknown

A bridegroom is a man who has just lost his self-control. Unknown

A bridegroom is a man who has lost his liberty in the pursuit of happiness. Unknown

A bridegroom is the man who is never important at a wedding unless he fails to show up. Unknown

It is better to marry than burn. The Bible

Marriage is the intermission between the wedding and the divorce. Unknown

A fortune-hunter is man who marries money and soon finds out he has married something else that talks. Unknown

A fortune-hunter is man who isn't well off and seeks to marry a woman who is. Unknown

Marriage is one long conversation chequered by disputes. Robert Louis Stevenson

Don't be discouraged, because every wrong attempt discarded is another step forward. Fortune Cookie Wisdom

Next to no wife, a good wife is best. Thomas Fuller

Quotes on Sex, Love & Marriage

Getting married to a woman before making love to her is like buying someone's horse over the telephone. Robert Williams

A woman seldom asks advice before she has bought her wedding clothes. Joseph Addison

A false enchantment can all too easily last a lifetime. W.H. Auden

Concubinage has been corrupted by marriage. Friedrich Nietzsche

The honeymoon is the first rude awakening for the male as to which sex is really the stronger. Eugene Brussell

To marry is to get a binocular view of life. William Inge Longford

The happiness of a married man depends on the people he has not married. Oscar Wilde

Marriage is hardly a thing one can do now and then - except in America. Oscar Wilde

A fortune-hunter is a man who never marries until he meets the right amount. Unknown

A fortune-hunter is a man who marries a woman for her figure, especially when the figure runs into the millions. Unknown

Quotes on Sex, Love & Marriage

A gadabout is a creature who looks for a husband before marriage, and whose husband looks for her afterward. Unknown.

A GI is a young American whose combat training in the Army prepares him for marriage. Unknown

A gold digger is the kind of woman who is just as willing to marry a man for his money as to divorce him for it. Unknown

An heiress is a girl who can support a husband and who doesn't have much trouble finding a husband to support. Unknown

A groom is a man who's fit to be tied - down. Unknown

A debutante is a girl with finance looking for a fiance'. Unknown

Courtship is the period during which a man spends so much on his girlfriend that he finally marries her for his money. Unknown

A bachelor is one who never got around to marrying in his youth, but has gotten around it ever since. Unknown

A coed is a girl who sometimes marries to escape school, only to find her education just beginning. Unknown

Quotes on Sex, Love & Marriage

A bachelor believes that romance brings out the best in a woman, while marriage brings out the worst. Unknown

The diamond is the stone upon which the foundation of marriage is often built. Unknown

A bachelor is a man who doesn't want to get married because he already has a boss he's working for. Unknown

Courtship is a game of cards where a girl has a heart and a man takes it with a diamond, and then her hand is his. Unknown

A diamond is a very hard jewel that will cut into anything, especially a young man's savings. Unknown

A groom is a person associated with brides and bridles. Unknown

Quotes on Sex, Love & Marriage

Quotes on Women

We owe a lot to daytime TV. Think of all the women who might otherwise be out driving. Unknown

An old maid is a lemon that has never been squeezed. Unknown

For a single woman, preparing for company means wiping the lipstick off the milk carton. Elayne Boosler

Never trust a woman with a man's voice. French Proverb

The easiest kind of relationship for me is with ten thousand people. The hardest is with one. Joan Baez

A well adjusted woman is one who not only knows what she wants for her birthday, but what she's going to exchange it for. Unknown

I'm selfish, impatient and a little insecure. I make mistakes, I am out of control and at times hard to handle. But if you can't handle me at my worst, then you sure as hell don't deserve me at my best. Marilyn Monroe

There's nothing a wife loves more than a double chin on her husband's old girlfriend. Unknown

Quotes on Sex, Love & Marriage

Next to God, we are indebted to women, first for life itself, and then for making it worth having. Bovee

Any girl can be glamorous, all you have to do is stand still and look stupid. Hedy Lamar

Women like to sit down with trouble as if it were knitting. Ellen Glasgow

You'd be surprised how much it costs to look this cheap. Dolly Parton

Women always speak the truth, but not the whole truth. Italian Proverb

The most subtle flattery a woman can receive is that conveyed by actions, not by words. Mad. Neckar

A woman is like a tea bag. You don't know her strength until she is in hot water. Nancy Reagan

Strength is the capacity to break a chocolate bar into four pieces with your bare hands, and then eat just one of the pieces. Judith Viorst

The years that a woman subtracts from her age are not lost. They are added to the ages of other women. Diane de Poitiers

Sensibility is the power of woman. Lavater

Quotes on Sex, Love & Marriage

Girls who eat sweets take up two seats. Unknown

Anything you tell a woman usually goes in one ear and out to the neighbors. Unknown

A smart female is one who quits playing ball when she makes a good catch. Unknown

Give a woman a job and she grows balls. Jack Gelber

She is like the rest of the women - thinks two and two'll come to make five, if she cries and bothers enough about it. George Eliot

Whatever women do they must do twice as well as men to be thought half as good. Luckily, this is not difficult. Charlotte Whitton

No woman objects to being called intelligent provided she is assured that it has done no harm to her looks. Aubrey Menen

The only secret a woman can keep is the one she doesn't know. Arab Proverb

I refuse to admit I'm more than fifty-two even if that does make my sons illegitimate. Lady Astor

Actresses don't have husbands, they have attendants. Margaret Anglin

Quotes on Sex, Love & Marriage

Brigands demand your money or your life; women require both. Nicholas Butler

There's nothing so cold as a woman who's been refused a fur coat. Unknown

Most every woman's age is like the speedometer on a used car, you know it's set back but you don't know how far. Unknown

A girdle doesn't change a woman's weight. It only moves it to a more interesting location. Unknown

The fickleness of the women I love is only equaled by the constancy of the women who love me. George Bernard Shaw

A good many women are good tempered simply because it saves the wrinkles coming too soon. Baroness Von Hutten

The chief excitement in a woman's life is spotting women who are fatter than she is. Helen Rowland

Resolved, that the women of this nation in 1876, have greater cause for discontent, rebellion and revolution that the men of 1776. Susan B. Anthony

Pity is the deadliest feeling that can be offered to a woman. Vicki Baum

Quotes on Sex, Love & Marriage

I never hated a man enough to give him his diamonds back. Zsa Zsa Gabor

A woman's word is never done. American Proverb

One woman's poise is another woman's poison. Katherine Brush

The way to a woman's heart is through your wallet. Frank Dane

A woman's mind is cleaner than a man's; she changes it more often. Oliver Herford

A woman is a person who knows fifty-nine different ways of saying no when she consents to something. Unknown

A temporary atheist is a woman who hasn't won at bingo in three weeks. Unknown

A woman has reached middle age when her girdle pinches and the men don't. Unknown

The only person who listens to both sides of an argument is the woman in the next apartment. Unknown

The modern rule is that every woman must be her own chaperone. Amy Vanderbilt

Quotes on Sex, Love & Marriage

It takes all the fun out of a bracelet if you have to buy it yourself. Peggy Joyce

No woman is too bashful to talk scandal. Dutch Proverb

A woman is a creature whose legs are longer than her stockings, and her feet are bigger than her shoes. Unknown

Trousers are a garment like jeans, worn by women who like it tight, or slacks, worn by women who like it loose. Unknown

Venal is the woman whose favorite beast of burden is the man who is loaded with money. Unknown

A wallflower is the girl who wears a sweater to keep warm. Unknown

Wiles are womaneuvers. Unknown

A window-shopper is a woman who probably has no more room in her clothes closets. Unknown

To rescue, to revenge, to instruct or to protect a woman, is all the same as to love her. Richter

The happiest women, like the happiest nations, have no history. George Eliot

The laughter of girls is, and ever was, among the delightful sounds of earth. De Quincey

Quotes on Sex, Love & Marriage

Kindness in women, not their beauteous looks, shall win my love. Shakespeare

A woman who we truly love is a religion. Emile de Girardin

A woman's tongue is only three inches long, but it can kill a man six feet high. Japanese Proverb

Trustworthy is the woman who can be trusted with a secret, because she never tells who told her. Unknown

Truthful is the woman who never lies about anything except her age, her weight and her husband's salary. Unknown

A woman is a creature who will sometimes use a hammer to drive in a nail but who usually prefers a hairbrush. Unknown

Talk to me tenderly, tell me lies; I am a woman and time flies. Vivian Yeiser Laramore

Women give themselves to God when the devil wants nothing more to do with them. Sophie Arnould

Big girls don't cry, big girls have alibis. Marilyn J. Williams

From birth to eighteen, a girl needs good parents. From eighteen to thirty-five, she needs good looks. From thirty-five to fifty-five, she needs a good personality. From fifty-five on, she needs good cash. Sophie Tucker

Quotes on Sex, Love & Marriage

There are no good girls gone wrong. There are just girls found out. Mae West

When a woman has no answer, the sea is empty of water. German Proverb

We women do talk too much, but even then we don't tell half we know. Lady Nancy Astor

Women love the lie that saves their pride, but never an unflattering truth. Gertrude Atherton

If a woman looks at her watch, it is a sure sign that someone is in the way. Shelland Bradley

Women are such expensive things. George Meredith

Friendship among women is only a suspension of hostilities. Comte de Rivarol

A woman is a person whose promise to be on time carries a lot of wait. Unknown

A woman is a creature made before mirrors, and who has been before them ever since. Unknown

Ladies of fashion starve their happiness to feed their vanity, and their love to feed their pride. Colton

Quotes on Sex, Love & Marriage

Woman is a calamity, but every house must have it's curse.
Arabian Proverb

The wants of women are an unknown quantity. A. Rhodes

A woman is a person who never knows her worst fault until she quarrels with her best friend. Unknown

A paradox is the woman who never knows what she wants, yet usually manages to get it. Unknown

Pregnancy is the only time when a woman wishes she were a year older. Unknown

Punctuality is the feminine art of knowing when to be late only at the right time. Unknown

Reasonable is what a woman is if she isn't always unreasonable. Unknown

A show-off is the woman who will wear anything to attract attention, even sensible clothes. Unknown

A snob is a woman who was born with her face lifted.
Unknown

A shrew is a woman who makes up her mind more often than she makes up her face. Unknown

Quotes on Sex, Love & Marriage

A snob is an aloof woman who never associates with her inferiors, if she can find any. Unknown

A sourpuss is the woman on whom face cream curdles. Unknown

A snob is the woman who greets you with an icy smile followed by a few well-frozen words. Unknown

A paradox is the woman who spends money on sheer stockings that make her look bare-legged. Unknown

A woman is a person who is expensive when picked up, and explosive when dropped. Unknown

No matter how happily a woman may be married, it always pleases her to discover that there is a nice man who wishes she were not. H.L. Mencken

A teenager is a girl in her teens who dresses like twelve and acts like twenty. Unknown

A true shopper is the woman who spends half her time buying things, and the other half returning them. Unknown

A shopper is a creature who spends the first part of her life shopping for a husband, and the rest of her life shopping for everything else. Unknown

Quotes on Sex, Love & Marriage

Few girls are as well shaped as a good horse. Christopher Morley

Women are most fascinating between the age of thirty-five and forty after they have won a few races and know how to pace themselves. Since few women ever pass forty, maximum fascination can continue indefinitely. Christian Dior

A fashionable woman is always in love - with herself. La Rochefoucauld

As soon as Eve ate the apple of wisdom, she reached for the fig leaf; when a woman begins to think, her first thought is of a new dress. Heinrich Heine

Shopping is what a woman does to see if she can find anything to make her want something. Unknown

A teenage girl is one who pretends to be shocked when she's not, or pretends not to be shocked when she is. Unknown

A tomboy is the youngster who hasn't yet discovered that a girl's strength lies in her weakness. Unknown

In the theater, a hero is one who believes that all women are ladies, a villain one who believes that all ladies are women. George Jean Nathan

If God had to give a woman wrinkles, He might at least have put them on the soles of her feet. Ninon de Lenclos

Quotes on Sex, Love & Marriage

Music and women I cannot but give way to, whatever my business is. Samuel Pepys

Where is any author in the world teaches such beauty as a woman's eye? Shakespeare

It is easier for a woman to defend her virtue against men than her reputation against women. French Proverb

Thirty is the age when a woman stops counting years and starts counting calories. Unknown

A sweet tooth is the reason why some girls eat a lot of sweets and soon develop bigger seats. Unknown

Sympathy is what one girl offers another in exchange for the details. Unknown

A corset is a garment worn by a woman to keep her overweight undercover. Unknown

A confidante is the friend to whom a woman first tells a secret. Unknown

A slanderer is the woman who lowers her voice while talking to another woman who raises her eyebrows while listening. Unknown

Quotes on Sex, Love & Marriage

A smile is what the best dressed woman always wears. Unknown

A snob is a woman with an icy manner who deserves to be defrosted constantly. Unknown

A spa is a place where women spend time increasing expenses by reducing expanses. Unknown

A spinster is a woman who missed the opportunity of being divorced. Unknown

A spitfire is the woman who loses her head easily and never misses it. Unknown

Teenage is the period when a girl is all skin and phones. Unknown

I make presents to the mother, but think of the daughter. Goethe

A woman forgives only when she is in the wrong. Arsene Houssaye

Women's intuition is the result of millions of years of not thinking. Rupert Hughes

She has a nice sense of rumor. John H. Cutler

Quotes on Sex, Love & Marriage

A snob is a woman who should have her nose lowered by a plastic surgeon. Unknown

Slacks are a garment worn by many a woman whose end doesn't justify jeans. Unknown

A confidante is the woman who listens more secrets out of you than you intended to tell. Unknown

A coed is a girl who would rather be well-formed than well-informed. Unknown

A capacity for self-pity is one of the last things that any woman surrenders. Irvin S. Cobb

Virtue in women is often merely love of their reputation and of their peace of mind. La Rouchefoucauld

Women cure all their sorrows by talking. Jean Paul Richter

The rich widow cries with one eye and laughs with the other. Thomas Fuller

A woman on time is one in nine. Addison Mizner

I have no other but a woman's reason; I think him so because I think him so. William Shakespeare

A confidante is the trusted friend who will not give your secrets away, but will trade them for others. Unknown

Quotes on Sex, Love & Marriage

A cosmetician proves that one woman's fortune is another woman's face. Unknown

The romantic is the sentimental woman who cures her broken heart by getting it broken again. Unknown

A scandalmonger is a woman who is most happy when confessing the sins of other women. Unknown

A prude is a woman who blushes to listen and listens to blush. Unknown

A rag is any dress that a woman doesn't care to wear any more. Unknown

A rarity is the woman who can find something in her handbag on the first dive. Unknown

The divorcee is like a side dish that nobody remembers having ordered. Alexander King

A pretty country retreat is like a pretty wife, one is always throwing away money decorating it. Washington Irving.

I never knew a girl who was ruined by a book. James J. Walker

Here's to good old Whiskey
So amber and clear,
'Tis not so sweet as woman's lips

Quotes on Sex, Love & Marriage

But a damned sight more sincere. Lewis C. Henry

A racetrack is another place where a woman's intuition never seems to work. Unknown

A secret is what a woman tells everybody not to tell anybody. Unknown

As long as a woman can look ten years younger than her own daughter, she is perfectly satisfied. Oscar Wilde

One should never trust a women who tells her real age. If she tells that she'll tell anything. Oscar Wilde

There are two ways to handle a woman, and nobody knows either of them. Kin Hubbard

A secret is what a woman cannot keep or let anyone else keep. Unknown

A scatterbrain is a woman who, when her mind wanders, hasn't far to go. Unknown

A costume is an outer set of clothes worn by a woman to match her accessories. Unknown

A corset is another thing that gives till it hurts. Unknown

A woman repeats a secret because she doesn't know what else to do with it. Unknown

Quotes on Sex, Love & Marriage

Admiration is like champagne to a woman. The more she gets the more she wants. W. Burton Baldry

A woman will buy anything she thinks the store is loosing money on. Kin Hubbard

Rich widows are the only second-hand goods that sell at first class prices. Benjamin Franklin

Eve ate the apple, that she might dress. Douglas Jerrold

It is rare that, after having given the key of her heart, a woman does not change the lock the day after. Charles Beuve

I don't know of anything better than a woman if you want to spend money where it'll show. Kin Hubbard

One tongue is sufficient for a woman. John Milton

A secret is something that any woman can keep to herself - till she meets another woman. Unknown

A sentimentalist is the woman who ties her gifts with heartstrings. Unknown

Shopworn is the woman who has been shopping all day, and is tired and spent. Unknown

Quotes on Sex, Love & Marriage

The only way to understand a woman is to love her; and then it isn't necessary to understand her. Sydney Harris

A secret is one thing a woman cannot keep because it is either not good enough to keep or too good to keep. Unknown

Of all the calamities that befall mortal man, nothing is worse, or ever will be worse, than woman. Sophocles

If you want to know how old a woman is, ask her sister-in-law. Edgar Howe

When women kiss it always reminds me of prize fighters shaking hands. H.L. Mencken

Woman is the heart of humanity. Samuel Smiles

What keeps lovers and mistresses from tiring of being together is that they talk of nothing but themselves. LaRochefoucauld

She looks too lovely to be quite a lady. Samuel Hopkins Adams

The woman that deliberates is lost. Joseph Adsison

What a woman wants is what you're out of. O. Henry

Temptations are like women: he who knows one has they key for understanding all. Desmond Coke

Quotes on Sex, Love & Marriage

Girls who wear zippers shouldn't live alone. John Van Drutten

You love your automatic mouth;
  You love it's giddy whirl;
You love its fluent flow;
  You love to wind your mouth up;
You love to hear it go! Representative Marriot Brosius

The best way to get a woman to listen is to whisper. Stan Burns

When a man dies, the last thing that moves is his heart; in a woman her tongue. George Chapman

An honest woman is necessarily a married woman. Honore de Balzac

A sentimentalist is the woman whose heart is always going to her head. Unknown

A woman will always sacrifice herself if you give her the opportunity. It's her favorite form of self-indulgence. W. Somerset Maugham

It's not only important to add years to your life, but to add life to your years. Fortune Cookie Wisdom

Mirages are like women-strictly unpredictable. They always look inviting, cool and attractive, but you can't pin one down. Harry Oliver

Quotes on Sex, Love & Marriage

Women disregard the laws of their mind and heart if their temperaments rule otherwise. LaRochefoucauld

If a woman has all she wants of a thing, she doesn't want it. G.B. Burgin

Why is the word "tongue" feminine in Greek, Latin, Italian, Spanish, French, and German? Austin O'Malley

Society ladies are the most notable works of art in our modern galleries-they are painted well. J.M. Stuart-Young

Take the honorable path and you cannot go wrong. Fortune Cookie Wisdom

Two women placed together makes cold weather. Shakespeare

A woman without a laugh in her is the greatest bore in existence. William Thackeray

A secret is the only thing a woman gets just as much pleasure in giving as receiving. Unknown

The light ones may be killers,
  And the dark ones may be mild;
Not the wrappers, but the fillers,
  Make cigars or women wild. Keith Preston

Quotes on Sex, Love & Marriage

In a way an umpire is like a woman. He makes quick decisions, never reverses them, and doesn't think you're safe when you're out. Larry Goetz

Women often wish to give unwillingly what they really like to give. Ovid

Woman is as false as a feather in the wind. F.M. Piave

Charm is something a woman loses when she begins to count on it. Unknown

Furniture is another thing a woman likes to push around. Unknown

A gadabout is a woman who marries in order to have a home to get away from. Unknown

A gadabout is a woman who was born with the roaming instinct instead of the homing instinct. Unknown

A grandmother is the only woman who takes your side more often than your own mother. Unknown

A gossip is a woman who spends half her times talking to neighbors about friends, and the other half talking to friends about neighbors. Unknown

A gossip is a woman who always chooses someone more interesting than herself to talk about. Unknown

Quotes on Sex, Love & Marriage

A girdle is a woman's undergarment worn to take the middle out of middle age. Unknown

A gold digger is a minx who is after minks. Unknown

A girl is a creature who in childhood never hangs up her clothes, and in adolescence never hangs up the phone. Unknown

Girls are what women over forty call one another. Unknown

A gold digger is a woman without principle who draws a lot of interest. Unknown

A gold digger is a member of the tender gender always after the legal tender. Unknown

A gossip is a person who finds no one so annoying as the woman who never talks about anyone. Unknown

Greedy is the woman who in childhood never got enough dolls and who now cannot get enough dollars. Unknown

A hairdo is something on a woman's head that's even more changeable than what's one her mind. Unknown

The contents of a woman's purse is the best proof that money isn't everything. Unknown

Quotes on Sex, Love & Marriage

The gadabout is the woman who believes that, be it ever so humble, there's no place like somewhere else. Unknown

A gadabout is the woman who was born away from home, married away from home, and lives most of the day away from home. Unknown

A charmer is a woman who is as likable as she is lookable. Unknown

A bargain hunter is a compulsive woman who has a need to buy things she has no need for. Unknown

The tongue is a woman's sword and she never lets it rust. Unknown

A sewing circle is a group of women who darn more husbands than sox. Unknown

A secretary must think like a man, act like a lady, look like a girl, and work like a dog. Unknown

Women do not believe everything they hear, but this doesn't prevent them from repeating it. Unknown

When a woman is in a train of thought someone is bound to get run down. Unknown

A blonde is the cross between a brunette and a drugstore. Unknown

Quotes on Sex, Love & Marriage

A beauty shop is the parlor where scandal fills the air, and the talk alone may curl your hair. Unknown

The beach is where women try to show everything but their age. Unknown

A charmer is a delightful girl who looks good enough to eat and dresses with taste. Unknown

A gadabout is a woman with an outgoing personality.
Unknown

A gadabout is a woman whose place is in the home - of some other woman. Unknown

Clothes are what women wear to attract men and distract other women. Unknown

A careerist is any female who finds it easier to get a job than a husband. Unknown

Brains is what a clever girl hides behind a low neckline.
Unknown

Clothes is the only subject of conversation among women that's more common than the weather. Unknown

A clothes closet is the proof that women as well as men are trying to conquer space. Unknown

Quotes on Sex, Love & Marriage

A girdle is a device bound to make a woman slimmer on the outside than she is on the inside. Unknown

A fortune-teller is a woman who has put her feminine intuition on a paying basis. Unknown

Flirtation is a feminine pastime where one woman's hobby is another woman's hubby. Unknown

Make decisions from the heart and use your head to make it work out. Fortune Cookie Wisdom

Flattery is the kind of praise that always delights a vain woman, but never surprises her. Unknown

Feminine logic is the woman's belief that she can make out a check to cover the difference when she's overdrawn. Unknown

An evening gown is a low-cut dress that a woman enjoys wearing even though her heart isn't in it. Unknown

An echo is the only thing that can cheat a woman out of the last word. Unknown

A debutante is a bareback with greenbacks. Unknown

The clothesline is where our grandmothers used to hang out. Unknown

Quotes on Sex, Love & Marriage

A clotheshorse is a woman who is never happy unless she has a lot of new clothes she is not wearing. Unknown

A diamond is a woman's idea of a stepping stone to success. Unknown

Flattery is a feminine trick that enables many a woman to keep a man from finding out how foolish she is. Unknown

A clotheshorse is the woman who has closets full of nothing to wear. Unknown

A charmer is the kind of woman who knows how to ask the kind of questions a man is able to answer. Unknown

A chatterbox is a woman who talks like a revolving door. Unknown

A woman who meditates alone meditates evil. Publilius Syrus

A good woman is a hidden treasure, one who finds one does well not to boast of it. LaRochefoucauld

Heav'n has no Rage like Love to hatred tur'd,
Nor Hell a Fury like a Woman scorn'd. Congreve

When a women writes her confession she is never further from the truth. James G. Huneker

Quotes on Sex, Love & Marriage

The only people that understand women are women. Jim Bishop

Two are better than one, but the man who said that did not know my sisters. Samuel Butler

I want to make a policy statement. I am unabashedly in favor of women. Lyndon B. Johnson

Coquettes go to great trouble to seem jealous of their lovers to hide the fact that they are envious of other women. LaRochefoucauld

It is never too late for a woman to keep an appointment. Unknown

A woman, generally speaking, is generally speaking. Unknown

If the hen did not cackle, no one would know what she had been doing. Unknown

It is better to dwell in the corner of a housetop than with a brawling woman in a wide house. The Bible

A woman reaches for a chair when she answers the telephone. Unknown

Quotes on Sex, Love & Marriage

The five worst infirmities that afflict the female are indocility, discontent, slander, jealousy and silliness. Confucian Marriage Manual

Women have a keen sense of humor. The more you humor them the better they like it. Unknown

A shoe manufacturer's ambition is to perfect for women some shoes that are larger inside than they are outside. Unknown

All wickedness is but little to the wickedness of a woman. The Bible

Tongue in the mouth of woman is one of God's less agreeable blunders. The Talmud

A damsel is a female who has devised more defensive plays than football coaches. Unknown

Her clothes are so designed that she is always seen in the best places. Unknown

High heels were invented by a woman who was kissed on the forehead. Unknown

There are three kinds of women. Those one cannot live without, those one cannot live with, and those one lives with. Unknown

Bad girl: a good girl found out. Unknown

Quotes on Sex, Love & Marriage

In telling her age a woman is often shy in more ways than one. Unknown

Woman: a person who will spend $20 on a beautiful slip and then be annoyed if it shows. Unknown

Maturity is the mental competence of a woman when she stops looking for the ideal man and starts looking for a husband. Unknown

Inquisitiveness is a feminine trait so common as to make a woman without curiosity a curiosity. Unknown

Horse sense is what keeps a woman from turning into a nag. Unknown

An heiress is the only woman whose money talks more than she does. Unknown

An heiress is a woman who doesn't complain about having to live within her husband's income. Unknown

A hostess is a woman who puts two and two together when she should keep them apart. Unknown

Intuition is guessing right. Unknown

A nightclub is the only place that is still open by the time some wives finish dressing. Unknown

Quotes on Sex, Love & Marriage

Naive is when a woman thinks her friends think she looks as young as they say she does. Unknown

A movie star is a screen actress whose favorite husband is the next one. Unknown

Mother is the name given to a woman who doesn't believe in contraception. Unknown

A miniskirt is a skirt worn when a girl wants to look halfway decent. Unknown

Lovelorn is the state of mind when a woman shows great ingenuity in making a fool of herself. Unknown

Kittenish is when a middle - aged woman who pretends to be young by acting childish. Unknown

Kittenish is the type of woman who tries to act in the present as she used to feel in the past. Unknown

Knitting is an occupation that gives women something to think about while talking. Unknown

A lady - in - waiting is the feminine of bachelor. Unknown

Makeup is something a girl finds easier to do with her face than with her mind. Unknown

Quotes on Sex, Love & Marriage

A mink coat is the exception to the rule that women hate to wear the same garment other women wear. Unknown

A movie star is the only woman who can keep a maid longer than a husband. Unknown

Ms. is the abbreviation for a female who is either a girl or a woman, married or unmarried, separated or divorced, remarried or widowed. Unknown

A movie star is a woman who won't stay single, and won't stay married either. Unknown

A nag is the woman whose tongue is sharper than her teeth. Unknown

Intuition is what makes a woman feel sure about something that she doesn't know for certain. Unknown

Middle age is the age when a woman is not quite old enough to admit she is that old. Unknown

A potbellied woman lives beyond her seams. Unknown

If you tempt a squirrel with a nut, be prepared to be bitten. Fortune Cookie Wisdom

Old age is a state of mind that a vain woman never reaches, an unhappy woman reaches too soon, and a wise woman at the right time. Unknown

Quotes on Sex, Love & Marriage

An old maid is an unmarried woman in the prim of life. Unknown

A preacher is the only man who can keep dozens of women quiet for an hour. Unknown

Quotes on Sex, Love & Marriage

Quotes on Men

A sexagenarian is a man in his sixties who begins to realize that his grandfather was not so old when he died at eighty. Unknown

Golf is a game in which a small ball is chased by a man who is to old to chase anything else. Unknown

Never slap a guy in the face when he's chewing tobacco. Unknown

Old age is when a pretty girl arouses memories instead of hope. Unknown

Guys who pinch pennies will never pinch chorus girls. Unknown

If you are living with a man, you don't have to worry about whether you should sleep with him after dinner. Stephanie Brush

Bachelor, a peacock; betrothed, a lion; married, a donkey. Spanish Proverb

A male gynecologist is like an auto mechanic who has never owned a car. Carrie Snow

Quotes on Sex, Love & Marriage

Men are like the earth and we are like the moon; we turn always one side to them and they think there is no other. Olive Schreiner

Even Sir Isaac Newton had to be hit on the head before he learned the law of gravity. Unknown

A young man is always surprised when he learns that other young men think his sister is beautiful. Unknown

A man advertised for a wife in the papers. He got eighteen hundred replies from men who said he could have theirs. Unknown

A man is one who snatches the first kiss, pleads for the second, demands the third, takes the fourth, accepts the fifth; and endures all the rest. Helen Rowland

I like Frenchmen very much, because even when they insult you they do it so nicely. Josephine Baker

I like men to behave like men - strong and childish. Francoise Sagan

A bachelor never quite gets over the idea that he is a thing of beauty and a boy forever. Helen Rowland

A jealous man always finds more than he looks for. Mlle. Scudery

Quotes on Sex, Love & Marriage

No one is so busy as the man with nothing to do. French Proverb

Women want mediocre men, and men are working hard to be as mediocre as possible. Margaret Mead

The softer a man's head, the louder his socks. Helen Rowland

Take your troubles like a man, blame them on your wife. Unknown

Men, in general, are but great children. Napoleon

A father's heart is tender, though the man's is made of stone. Young

Man is a reasoning rather than a reasonable animal. Alexander Hamilton

Whatever the mind of man can conceive and believe, it can achieve. Fortune Cookie Wisdom

Every man is a volume, if you know how to read him. Channing

When faith is lost, and honor dies, the man is dead. Whittier

Quotes on Sex, Love & Marriage

A doorman is a genius who can open the door of your car with one hand, help you in with the other, and still have one left for the tip. Dorothy Kilgallen

A fox is a wolf who sends flowers. Ruth Weston

A man loses his illusions first, his teeth second and his follies last. Helen Rowland

Very few men care to have the obvious pointed out to them by a woman. Mrs. Baillie Saunders

Well, time wounds all heels. Jane Ace

A woman-hater is the man who believes that everything you say to a woman will be used against you. Unknown

A woman-hater is a man who has made mistakes with women, but none so great as the mistake of having nothing to do with them. Unknown

Every man has his devilish moments. Lavater

To appreciate heaven 'tis good for a man to have some fifteen minutes of hell. Will Carleton

A grateful dog is better than an ungrateful man. Saadi

A man isn't poor if he can still laugh. Raymond Hitchcock

Quotes on Sex, Love & Marriage

Men of cold passions have quick eyes. Hawthorne

A womanizer is a man who has angles if a pretty girl has curves. Unknown

Thrashing is the best way to get all the wild oats out of some boys. Unknown

We have reason to believe that man first walked upright to free his hands for masturbation. Lily Tomlin

Tipsy is the man who is sober enough to know he's drunk. Unknown

A boy looks for a towel after washing to find out if his face is clean. Unknown

Vintage is the most important factor in a man's choice of wine, women, and song. Unknown

Whiskers are face fungus. Unknown

A widower is the only man whose late wife is no longer late. Unknown

When a man is wrapped up in himself, he makes a pretty small package. John Ruskin

A man is only as old as the woman he feels. Groucho Marx

Quotes on Sex, Love & Marriage

Men employ speech only to conceal their thoughts. Voltaire

Whiskey is the only enemy that man has succeeded in loving. Unknown

A taxi driver is the man who never worries about the things that go on behind his back. Unknown

A womanizer is the married man who is less a husband than an ex-bachelor. Unknown

When a man sits with a pretty girl for an hour, it seems like a minute. But let him sit on a hot stove for a minute - and it's longer than any hour. That's relativity. Albert Einstein

Men who are unhappy, like men who sleep badly, are always proud of the fact. Bertrand Russell

A good scare is worth more to a man than good advice. E.W. Howe

Old boys have their playthings as well as young ones; the difference is only in the price. Benjamin Franklin

Most men's anger about religion is as if two men should quarrel for a lady they neither of them care for. Lord Halifax

Biggest mystery to a married man is what a bachelor does with his money. Unknown

Quotes on Sex, Love & Marriage

Adolescence is the awkward age when a boy's voice and vice are changing. Unknown

A country club is the place where more good lies are heard around the bar than are seen on the golf course. Unknown

A fortune hunter is a generous man who is willing to give his name in exchange for her money. Unknown

A gentleman is a man who never contradicts a woman, sometimes out of courtesy but often out of cowardice. Unknown

A grouch is a man who feels dog tired at night because he growls all day. Unknown

A hairpiece is the proof that many a man attaches more importance to what's on his head than to what's in it. Unknown

A hangover is the proof that the higher a man feels in the evening, the lower he feels in the morning. Unknown

A sourpuss is a grouch with a permanent-press frown. Unknown

A stag party is an affair where a lot of men get together and stagnate for the lack of women. Unknown

Quotes on Sex, Love & Marriage

A souse is one who is always out of spirits between drinks.
Unknown

A gentleman is the man who is unaware that he is one.
Unknown

A fortune-hunter is a man who, if he can't get a rich wife will settle for a rich father-in-law. Unknown

A man of the world never runs after a bus or a woman, because another will be along shortly. Unknown

Male chauvinism is the contempt for the opposite sex by men who think they are the only ones who understand women.
Unknown

A lecher is a man who has angles because women have curves.
Unknown

An intellectual is a man who has found something more appealing than women. Unknown

A hospital is a place where there are always more male patients than patient males. Unknown

A hermit is the only man who is not on a mailing list.
Unknown

I drink to make other people interesting. George Jean Nathan

Quotes on Sex, Love & Marriage

Popularity is exhausting. The life of the party almost always winds up in a corner with an overcoat over him. Wilson Mizner

Whenever you see a man with handkerchief, socks and tie to match, you may be sure he is wearing a present. Frank Case

A highbrow is a man who has found something more interesting than women. Edgar Wallace

A hobbyist is the man who has found something more interesting than women. Unknown

A lecher is one who often courts trouble but seldom ends up marrying it. Unknown

A male chauvinist is one whose delusion is that there is more wrong with women than with him. Unknown

A man is the only creature vainer than a woman. Unknown

Man has imagined a heaven, and has left entirely out of it the supremest of all his delights...sexual intercourse!...His heaven is like himself: strange, interesting, astonishing, grotesque. I give you my word, it has not a single feature in it that he actually values. Mark Twain

Man is the only creature on earth who thinks he more sense than a woman. Unknown

Quotes on Sex, Love & Marriage

The male animal goes through a crisis at 14 when his voice changes, and through another at 40 when his choice changes. Unknown

A philanderer is a man with a built-in early-warning system. Unknown

A philanderer is an amorist to whom variety is the spice of love. Unknown

Night life is a matter mostly of wine, women, and aspirin. Unknown

Many men believe in monogamy because enough is enough. Unknown

Middle age is the period of your life when a girl you smile at thinks you know her. Unknown

A married man is one who cannot understand why all bachelors are not millionaires. Unknown

The golf course is the place where a man goes to putt away his troubles. Unknown

He is old enough to know worse. Oscar Wilde

A bachelor is a man who thinks the weekend is something you rest up in. Kenneth Kraft

Quotes on Sex, Love & Marriage

Adam was human; he didn't want the apple for the apple's sake; he wanted it because it was forbidden. Mark Twain

Nearly every man is a firm believer in heredity until his son makes a fool of himself. Herbert V. Prochnow

A married man knows that it's safer to tease a dog than a woman. Unknown

Nostalgia is going back to your old home and finding it wasn't your boyhood town you longed for, but your boyhood. Unknown

A philanderer is a man who first runs after a woman and then runs away. Unknown

A dandy is a dude who, after marriage, becomes subdued. Unknown

Dating is the game in which a young man tries to act old, and an old man tries to act young. Unknown

Dating is a game of stop and go in which some men don't know when to stop, and others don't know when to go. Unknown

Desertion is the act of a married man who never got over his desire to run away from home as a boy. Unknown

A fisherman finds it impossible to keep both hands in his pockets while describing the fish that got away. Unknown

Quotes on Sex, Love & Marriage

Peace of mind is the repose of the man who is too busy to worry by day, and too sleepy to worry at night. Unknown

A playboy is a man about town and a fool about women. Unknown

A practical joker is a man who shakes your hand one minute and pulls your leg the next. Unknown

A septuagenarian is a man whose get-up-and-go has got up and gone. Unknown

A show-off is a man easy to see through because he is always making a spectacle of himself. Unknown

A sinner is a man who avoids the straight and narrow path, probably because there's no place to park. Unknown

A playboy is a good liver who eventually gets a bad liver. Unknown

Fishing is the most enjoyable way to loaf without inviting criticism. Unknown

A philanderer is an amorist who becomes slap-happy before he reaches middle age. Unknown

A confirmed bachelor is a bachelor over forty, because before that age he is not confirmed, but merely obstinate. Unknown

Quotes on Sex, Love & Marriage

Consistent is the bachelor who always says no and never gets married, or the husband who always says yes and never gets divorced. Unknown

An entanglement is the difficulty of the womanizer who is involved with the woman he loves, the woman who loves him, and his wife. Unknown

A philanderer is a man who never bothered by temptation, except when he can't find any. Unknown

A playboy is a man who plays like a boy but not at the same games. Unknown

Money is an old man's sex appeal. Unknown

I know well what I am fleeing from but not what I am in search of. Michel de Montaigne

Middle age is the time when a man is always thinking that in a week or two, he will feel as good as ever. Don Marquis

A playboy is a rich man who prefers young mistresses to old masters. Unknown

A corkscrew is a device that opens the bottle before the bottle opens the man. Unknown

Quotes on Sex, Love & Marriage

A bachelor is a selfish, callous, undeserving man who has cheated some worthy woman out of a divorce. Unknown

College is a young man's interlude of freedom between subjection to his mother and submission to his wife. Unknown

A bachelor is an eligible man who usually has his hands full trying to loosen a woman's grip. Unknown

A philanderer is a man who would rather have a woman on his mind than on his back. Unknown

A burglar is another man who isn't as rich as he thinks he ought to be. Unknown

College is an institution full of young men who will make good first husbands. Unknown

A confirmed bachelor is a man with unalterable views. Unknown

Father is name for a man who doesn't practice birth control. Unknown

That man is richest whose pleasures are cheapest. Henry David Thoreau

Whenever a man's friends begin to compliment him about looking young, he may be sure that they think he is growing old. Washington Irving

Quotes on Sex, Love & Marriage

There is no man living who isn't capable of doing more than he thinks he can do. Henry Ford

I never trust a man unless I've got his pecker in my pocket. Lyndon B. Johnson.

A playboy is a man who always keeps to the same routine: wine, women, an' s'long. Unknown

A playboy is a wealthy man who winters in Florida, summers in Canada, and springs at blondes. Unknown

A bachelor is a conscientious objector in the war between the sexes. Unknown

Poker is a card game where the man with a vacant stare generally has a full house. Unknown

A priest is the only man who remains a bachelor no matter how many wives he marries. Unknown

A retiree is a man whose problem is how to spend a lot of time without spending a lot of money. Unknown

Salesmanship is treating your customer as if she were your best girl, not your wife. Unknown

A scatterbrain is a man who, when he looks confused, is probably thinking. Unknown

Quotes on Sex, Love & Marriage

Every man has his follies, and often they are the most interesting things he's got. Josh Billings

Boys will be boys, and so will a lot of middle-aged men. Kin Hubbard

A man is in general better pleased when he has a good dinner upon his table than when his wife talks Greek. Samuel Johnson

Biggest mystery to a bachelor is what happened to his money. Robert Williams

Confirmed bachelor: one who thinks that the only thoroughly justified marriage was the one that produced him. Harlan Miller

Many a man does not find his heart until he has lost his head. Friedrich Nietzsche

A retiree is the old-timer who had always worked hard without living and now finds it even harder to live without working. Unknown

A poker face is an expression by which a cardplayer conceals the kind of hand he has by the kind of face he hasn't. Unknown

Quotes on Sex, Love & Marriage

A little nonsense now and then is relished by the wisest men. Unknown

A man hath no better thing under the sun, than to eat, and to drink, and to be merry. The Bible

A rake is a lecher who won't hesitate to go around with a married woman even if he can't go two rounds with her husband. Unknown

Repartee is what a man thinks of on his way home. Unknown

Men are more loveable for the bad qualities they don't posses than for the good ones they do. E. Phillips Oppenheim

A man is never drunk if he can lay on the floor without holding on. Joe Lewis

Every man has a scheme that won't work. E.W. Howe

An optimist is a man who calls bullshit fertilizer. Frank Dane

A rascal is one who is very good at being no good. Unknown

A realist is a man who keeps both feet on the ground and still gets somewhere. Unknown

Gentlemen who prefer blondes usually marry brunettes. Unknown

Quotes on Sex, Love & Marriage

Bachelor: a man who, when he accomplishes something, gets all the credit himself. Unknown

A realist is a man who believes in doing it today because tomorrow there may be a law against it. Unknown

When a 220-pound man laughs, there is twice as much of him having a good time as when a 110-pound man laughs. This is one of the advantages of being fat. Hal Boyle

He that drinks well, sleeps well. Thomas Wilson

Always remember, that I have taken more out of alcohol than alcohol has taken out of me. Sir Winston Churchill

The man who lives free from folly is not so wise as he thinks. LaRochefoucauld

I've always been given to understand that men only abandon their vices when advancing years have made them a burden rather than a pleasure. W. Somerset Maugham

A man, to be great, must know how to make the most of all his chances. LaRochefoucauld

Men often oppose a thing, merely because they have had no agency in planning it, or because it may have been planned by those whom they dislike. Hamilton

Quotes on Sex, Love & Marriage

How is it possible for a man to have his ear to the ground, his head in the clouds, and still have his foot in his mouth?
Unknown

Happiness is a mental state aided by wine, women and tobacco.
Unknown

Men who complain that the boss is dumb would be out of a job if he were any smarter. Unknown

Character is what a man is in the dark. Unknown

I have noticed that nothing I never said ever did me any harm.
Calvin Coolidge

One of the oldest and quietest roads to contentment lies through the conventional Trinity of wine, women, and song.
Rexford Guy Tugwell

Many a man's tongue broke his nose. Seumas MacManus

I want what I want when I want it! Henry Blossom

A man has more fun wishing for the things he hasn't got than enjoying the things he has got. Finley Peter Dunne

Lucky men seldom mend their ways; they always feel in the right so long as luck favors their ill behavior.
LaRochefoucauld

Quotes on Sex, Love & Marriage

Quotes on Women & Men

Finesse is the artfulness of a girl to make a slow man think he's a fast worker. Unknown

The human male is the only animal from eight to eighty always has to explain to some woman why he didn't come home earlier. Unknown

Middle age is the period when, if you go all out, you end up all in. Unknown

A playboy is a womanizer with money to burn who pursues girls willing to play with fire. Unknown

An old fogy is one who disapproves of slacks for women because woman's place is in the home and not in men's pants. Unknown

I am a marvelous housekeeper. Every time I leave a man I keep his house. Zsa Zsa Gabor

He promised me earrings, but he only pierced my ears. Arabian Proverb

A man who was loved by 300 women singled me out to live with him. Why? I was the only one without a cat. Elayne Boosler

Quotes on Sex, Love & Marriage

One of the advantages of living alone is that you don't have to wake up in the arms of a loved one. Marion Smith

Outside every thin woman is a fat man trying to get in. Katherine Whitehorn

An old maid is person of either sex who is prickly, prissy and proper. Unknown

Never fear! The end of something is the start of something new. Fortune Cookie Wisdom

A playgirl is a playmate in search of a paymate. Unknown

Middle age is ten years older than you are. Unknown

Men's vows are women's traitors. Shakespeare

A woman is a woman until the day she dies, but a man's a man only as long as he can. Moms Mabley

The quarrels of lovers are like summer storms. Everything is more beautiful when they have passed. Mad. Necker

A hundred men may make an encampment, but it takes a woman to make a home. Chinese Proverb

A woman's head is always influenced by heart; but a man's heart by his head. Lady Blessington

Quotes on Sex, Love & Marriage

To a woman the first kiss is just the end of the beginning; to a man it is the beginning of the end. Helen Rowland

The vows that woman makes to her fond lover are only fit to be written on air, or on the swiftly passing stream. Catullus

The whole world is strewn with snares, traps, gins and pitfalls for the capture of men by women. George Bernard Shaw

A husband is a plaster that cures all the ills of girlhood. Moliere

A flatterer is a person who is seldom interrupted. Unknown

Women of genius commonly have masculine faces, figures and manners. In transplanting brains to an alien soil God leaves a little of the original earth clinging to the roots. Benjamin Tucker

Contact with a high-minded woman is good for the life of any man. Henry Vincent

The happiest time in any man's life is just after the first divorce. John Kenneth Galbraith

Drying a widow's tears is one of the most dangerous occupations known to man. Dorothy Dix

Quotes on Sex, Love & Marriage

Men always fall for frigid women because they put on the best show. Fanny Brice

God sent us women, and the Devil sent them corsets. French Proverb

A fool and her money are soon courted. Helen Rowland

The female of the species is more deadly than the male. Rudyard Kipling

God created man, and, finding him not sufficiently alone, gave him a female companion to make him feel his solitude more keenly. Paul Valery

On one issue at least, men and women agree, they both distrust women. H.L. Mencken

Flattery is the best cure for a stiff neck because there are few heads it won't turn. Unknown

Flattery is the compliment a woman remembers long after she has forgotten the name of the man who paid it. Unknown

A flirt is the woman without a heart who makes a fool of the man without a head. Unknown

Marriage is a custom that will never go out of style because the wiles of women are stronger than the wills of men. Unknown

Quotes on Sex, Love & Marriage

A gossip is one who gets her best news from somebody who promised to keep it a secret. Unknown

A flirt is a woman who makes some men forget they are married, and makes others remember it only too well. Unknown

It's tough to be fascinating. Fortune Cookie Wisdom

Gallantry to women, the sure road to their favor, is nothing but the appearance of extreme devotion to all their wants and wishes, a delight in their satisfaction, and a confidence in yourself as being able to contribute toward it. Hazlitt

The reason that husbands and wives do not understand each other is because they belong to different sexes. Dorothy Dix

A coquette is a woman without any heart, who makes a fool of a man that hasn't got any head. Mme. Deluzy

Lying is a fault in a boy, an art in a lover, an accomplishment in a bachelor, and second nature in a married woman. Helen Rowland

Women resist in order to be conquered. Italian Proverb

A bachelor is one who gets tangled up with a lot of women in order to avoid getting tied up to one. Helen Rowland

Quotes on Sex, Love & Marriage

A flirt is woman who feels she might just as well make a fool out of a man as to let some other woman do it. Unknown

Marriage is an experience that turns the man who thinks he knows about women into a man who doesn't know what to think. Unknown

A diamond is a gem whose bright sparkle renders a woman stone-blind to the man offering it. Unknown

Divorce court is an institution whose aim is to stop a man from continuing to cheat on his wife. Unknown

Equal rights is letting the girl pay the check when she is out with a man. Unknown

Conversation between Adam and Eve must have been difficult at times because they had nobody to talk about. Agnes Repplier

One man's folly is another man's wife. Helen Rowland

What could Adam have done to God that made Him put Eve in the garden? Polish Proverb

I don't mind living in a man's world as long as I can be a woman in it. Marilyn Monroe

Quotes on Sex, Love & Marriage

A good woman inspires a man, a brilliant woman interests him, a beautiful woman fascinates him - the sympathetic woman gets him. Helen Rowland

Women prefer men who have something tender about them - especially the legal kind. Kay Ingram

Faith is a woman's trust in a man when she knows he isn't to be trusted. Unknown

A diversion is what shopping is to the woman who hasn't bought a thing, or fishing is to the man who hasn't caught a thing. Unknown

Love lessens woman's delicacy, and increases man's. Richter

It is not decided that women love more than men, but it is indisputable that they love better. Dubay

In all societies women have played a much more important role than their menfolk are generally ready to admit. Ashley Montagu

Why is the husband who constantly complains he can't get a word in edgewise always so hoarse? Peggy Weidman

There are very few jobs that actually require a penis or a vagina. All other jobs should be open to everybody. Florence Kennedy

Quotes on Sex, Love & Marriage

I'm glad I am not a man, for if I were I would be obligated to marry a woman. Madame de Stael

With a woman, first thoughts are best; with a man, second thoughts. Italian Proverb

Love, the quest; marriage, the conquest; divorce, the inquest. Helen Rowland

I always say, keep a diary and some day it will keep you. Mae West

A bachelor has to have inspiration for making love to a woman, a married man needs only an excuse. Helen Rowland

The sexes were made for each other, and only in the wise and loving union of the two is the fulness of health and duty and happiness to be expected. W. Hall

Women detest a jealous man whom they do not love, but it angers them when a man they do love is not jealous. L'Enclos

People are lonely because they build walls instead of bridges. Joseph Fort Newton

The treasures of the deep are not so precious as are the concealed comforts of a man locked up in woman's love. Middleton

Quotes on Sex, Love & Marriage

Faux pas is telling a woman that something is as plain as the nose on her face. Unknown

Purity is the feminine, truth the masculine of honor. Hare

Throughout history females have picked providers, males have picked anything. Margaret Mead

Before marriage a man will lie awake all night thinking about something you said; after marriage he'll fall asleep before you finish saying it. Helen Rowland

It's a sad house where the hen crows louder than the cock. Scottish Proverb

When women go wrong, men go right after them. Mae West

A wise man in the company of those who are ignorant, has been compared to a beautiful girl in the company of blind men. Saadi

A fool is the man who thinks he cannot do without women, or the woman who thinks she do without men. Unknown

A fortune-teller is one who tells an unmarried woman there's a man in her future, and tells a married woman there's a future in her man. Unknown

A friend is a person who goes around saying nice things behind your back. Unknown

Quotes on Sex, Love & Marriage

Frustration is what happens to the girl who marries a night owl in the hope of turning him into a homing pigeon. Unknown

A fur coat is something given to a woman to keep her warm or quiet. Unknown

A gentleman is a courteous man who always looks up to women, but never from a seat in a bus. Unknown

A gold digger is a woman who has what it takes to take what you have. Unknown

A woman who has never seen her husband fishing doesn't know what a patient man she has married. Ed Howe

The reason flattery makes people feel good is because they know they deserve it. Dr. Laurence Peter

You can be sincere and still be stupid. Charles Kettering

When a man confronts catastrophe on the road, he looks in his purse, but a woman looks in her mirror. Margaret Turnbull

Woman's virtue is man's greatest invention. Cornelia Otis Skinner

The average man is more interested in a woman who is interested in him than he is in a woman, any woman, with beautiful legs. Marlene Dietrich

Quotes on Sex, Love & Marriage

Never trust a husband too far, nor a bachelor too near. Helen Rowland

A quarrel between man and wife is like cutting water with a sword. Chinese Proverb

How it rejoices a middle-aged woman when her husband criticizes a pretty girl. Mignon McLaughlin

The only real happy folk are married women and single men. H.L. Mencken

Most after dinner speakers are men. Women can't wait that long. Unknown

Just because you put tap dance shoes on an elephant does not mean it can dance. Fortune Cookie Wisdom

Women are getting men's wages now - but then, they always have. Unknown

True friendship comes when silence between two people is comfortable. Dave Tyson Gentry

Coquetry is the gentle art of making a man feel pleased with himself. Helen Rowland

Quotes on Sex, Love & Marriage

Here's to man, he can afford anything he can get. Here's to woman, she can afford anything she can get a man to get for her. George Ade

It is a profound truth that women as a sex are vain; it is also a profound truth that men as a sex are vain. Arnold Bennett

What man wants: all he can get; what woman wants: all she can't get. George D. Prentice

The only way a woman can ever reform a man is by boring him so completely that he loses all possible interest in life. Oscar Wilde

In the garden of Eden sat Adam
Disporting himself with his madam.
   She was filled with elation,
   For in all of creation
There was only one man - and she had'm. Unknown

Up to sixteen a lad is a Boy Scout. After that he is a girl scout. Unknown

A bachelor is one who enjoys the chase but does not eat the game. Unknown

A beautiful woman can get almost anything except your point of view. Unknown

Quotes on Sex, Love & Marriage

What every girl should know: a millionaire bachelor.
Unknown

A virus is something originated by a doctor whose wife wanted a mink coat. Unknown

A smart man is one who hasn't let a woman pin anything on him since he was a baby. Unknown

Imagination: something that sits up with a woman when her husband comes home late. Unknown

When a woman tells you her age, it's alright to look surprised, but don't scowl. Wilson Mizner

After having lived half their lives respectably, many men get tired of honesty, and many women of propriety. Sydney Smith

Women like silent men. They think they're listening. Marcel Achard

Mouth: in man, the gateway to the soul; in woman, the outlet of the heart. Ambrose Bierce

Men have more problems than women. In the first place, they have to put up with women. Francoise Sagan

With a man a lie is a last resort; with women, its first aid.
Gelett Burgess

Quotes on Sex, Love & Marriage

Night Club: a place where the tables are reserved and the guests are not. Unknown

All human actions have one or more of these seven causes: chance, nature, compulsion, habit, reason, passion, desire. Unknown

The person who has learned to take things as they come, and to let go as they depart, has mastered one of the arts of cheerful and contented living. Unknown

It's wise to apologize to a man if you're wrong - and to a woman if you're right. Unknown

Life has a way of evening up things. For every woman who makes a fool out of some man there's another who makes a man out of some fool. Unknown

Diamond's are a girl's best friend and dogs are a man's best friend. Now you know which sex has more sense. Unknown

Men's troubles are due to three things, women, money, and both. Unknown

Winston Churchill once was asked if he knew any professional women. he answered promptly, "I've never met any amateur ones." Unknown

Quotes on Sex, Love & Marriage

The only way a woman can provide for herself decently is to be good to some man that can afford to be good to her. George Bernard Shaw

Man weeps to think that he will die so soon; woman, that she was born so long ago. H.L. Mencken

Man has his will, but woman has her way. Oliver Wendell Holmes

Man is always looking for something to boast to; woman is always looking for a shoulder to put her head on. H.L. Mencken

A lady doing her Christmas shopping asked a clerk, "What can you suggest for a man of fifty?" The clerk answered, "A girl of eighteen." Unknown

Life is like a dogsled team. If you ain't the lead dog, the scenery never changes. Fortune Cookie Wisdom

The head of the auto license bureau received his first thank you card in the mail the other day. It was the from the husband of a woman he'd flunked. Unknown

If you want to change a woman's mind, agree with her. Unknown

Nobody wants to hear your troubles, unless there's a woman involved. Unknown

Quotes on Sex, Love & Marriage

What men, in their egoism, constantly mistake for a deficiency of intelligence in woman is merely an incapacity for mastering that mass of small intellectual tricks, that complex of petty knowledge, that collection of rubber stamps, which constitutes the chief mental equipment of the average male. H.L. Mencken

The silliest woman can manage a clever man; but it needs a very clever woman to manage a fool. Rudyard Kipling

When a woman is speaking to you, listen to what she says with her eyes. Victor Hugo

It is a curious thing that when most women hate, they hate individuals and not people in mass. On the other hand, men frequently acquire a sort of abstract, mass hatred. W.E. Woodward

Bachelors know more about women than married men. If they didn't they'd be married too. H.L. Mencken

The husbands of the Ten Best-Dressed Women are never on the list of the Ten Best-Dressed Men. Unknown

The reason God made man before woman was because He didn't want any suggestions. Unknown

You can't shake hands with a clenched fist. Unknown

Quotes on Sex, Love & Marriage

When your wife goes along on a convention, you have twice the expenses and half the fun. Unknown

Nothing confuses a man more than driving behind a woman who does everything right. Unknown

Many women marry a man for life, and then discover he doesn't have any. Unknown

By the time a man can read women like a book he's too old to start a library. Unknown

I had made up my mind to stay home with her but she had her face made up to go out. Unknown

First I couldn't get her off my mind, now I can't get her off my hands. Unknown

An optimist is a man who thinks a woman will hang up the phone just because she said good-by. Unknown

Sex, according to old man Webster, is the difference between man and woman, and as long as there is man and woman, they will have their differences. Unknown

God made Adam for practice. Then He looked him over and said "I think I can do better than that," so he made Eve. Unknown

Woman is really spelled woe-man, you know. Unknown

Quotes on Sex, Love & Marriage

There are just as many husbands looking for girls as there are girls looking for husbands. Unknown

It is not true that woman was made from man's rib; she was really made from his funny bone. James Barrie

Girls are certainly the best idea that any boy has had to date. John Ciardi

Man's boldness and woman's caution make an excellent business arrangement. Elbert Hubbard

Many husbands are second story men - their wives seldom believe the first one. Frances Rodman

A woman may race to get a man a gift but it always ends in a tie. Earl Wilson

A zipper is the only thing that gets stuck on a woman more often than a man does. Unknown

A woman driver is a motorist who drives like a man, but gets criticized for it. Unknown

A womanizer is the philanderer who tries to get a girl's number before she gets his. Unknown

A siren is the kind of charmer a man likes to toast and a woman likes to roast. Unknown

Quotes on Sex, Love & Marriage

A shrew is a married woman who succeeds in breaking a man's will, sometimes after he dies, but more often before. Unknown

A shrewd wife is one who, as soon as her husband becomes used to her appearance, gets a new hairdo. Unknown

A skeptic is a man who thinks women cannot be trusted too far, or a woman who thinks men cannot be trusted too near. Unknown

A smart aleck is a young man who thinks he knows it all until some woman comes along and begins to educate him. Unknown

There never was a man who was not gratified by being told he was liked by the woman. Samuel Johnson

Men all want to be a woman's first love - women like to be a man's last romance. Oscar Wilde

When women have made a sheep of a man, they always tell him that he is a lion, with an iron will. Honore de Balzac

A man likes his wife to be just clever enough to understand his cleverness and just stupid enough to admire it. Israel Zangwill

Skepticism is the attitude of a woman when her husband tells the exact truth. Unknown

Quotes on Sex, Love & Marriage

A womanizer is a perfect gentleman who has to have his face slapped once in a while. Unknown

The women's liberation movement is a feminist movement whose members want to be liberated from men even before they have been captured by them. Unknown

A supermarket is the only place where men don't find fault with women drivers. Unknown

A virgin is a conscientious objector in the war between the sexes. Unknown

Woman is the best thing about man. Unknown

A woman is a creature less logical than a man but more biological. Unknown

A woman is one who is first busy picking up a husband, and then is busy picking on him. Unknown

A woman is a female who is either making a fool out of a man, or a making a man out of a fool. Unknown

The female of the species is smarter than the male because she never marries a dumb person on account of his shape. Unknown

Quotes on Sex, Love & Marriage

There's a difference between beauty and charm. A beautiful woman is one I notice. A charming woman is one who notices me. John Erskine

When a man buys a new hat, he wants one just like the one he has had before. But a woman isn't that way. E.W. Howe

The waistline is a line that fashion moves up or down for women, but expands only horizontally for men. Unknown

A man gets weak when a pretty girl tells him how strong he is. Unknown

A sophisticate is a man who, when he wants a girl to laugh at his jokes, tells her she has a musical laugh. Unknown

A gossip is a medium second only to the press in the dissemination of news. Unknown

A spinster is an elderly lady who refused to marry a man who lies. Unknown

Suspicion is what makes a very jealous woman investigate the past of her husband for future use. Unknown

Tears are what a woman resorts to when she wants to get something out of her system or out of her husband. Unknown

A two-timer is a slang term for the husband who shows his worst side to his better half. Unknown

Quotes on Sex, Love & Marriage

A widow is a woman who finds it easy to marry again because dead men tell no tales. Unknown

Once made equal to man, woman becomes his superior.
Socrates

Women lie about their age; men lie about their income.
William Feataher

Everyone is a moon and has a dark side which he never shows to anybody. Mark Twain

Unmarried is a woman who ran out of ammunition in the battle of the sexes. Unknown

Teenage is the period when girls begin to powder, and boys begin to puff. Unknown

A spinster is a woman with the cleanest mind who gives a philanderer the dirtiest looks. Unknown

A sophisticate is the girl who knows all the answers because she's been around with men who ask all the questions.
Unknown

A sourpuss is a disagreeable person who never wipes his opinion off his face. Unknown

Quotes on Sex, Love & Marriage

A spinster is the woman who couldn't stay awake while some man was talking about himself. Unknown

A diamond is the hardest substance for a woman to get, or for a man to get back. Unknown

A date is what a man breaks when he has to, and what a girl breaks when she has two. Unknown

A shellfish is another creature that has a crab for a mate. Unknown

A man buy shoes to fit his feet while a woman buys them to fit the occasion. Unknown

A shrew is the wife who corrects her husband's vision until he sees eye to eye with her. Unknown

A gossip is proof that nobody's business is everybody's curiosity. Unknown

Cosmetics are a form of chemical warfare used by women in the battle of the sexes. Unknown

I like men who have a future and women who have a past. Oscar Wilde

Henpecked is when the hens crow, and the cock holds his peace. John Florio

Quotes on Sex, Love & Marriage

A lady is a woman who makes a man behave like a gentleman. Russell Lynes

A shrew is the battle-ax who always wins the battle of the sexes. Unknown

There is no such thing as an old woman. Any woman of any age, if she loves, if she is good, gives a man a sense of the infinite. Jules Michelet

Nobody will ever win the Battle of the Sexes. There's just too much fraternizing with the enemy. Henry Kissenger

A shrew is a woman who is happily married as long as she has a husband who is scared to death of her. Unknown

Dancing is a skill in which the women know all the steps, and the men know the holds. Unknown

Cosmetics are beauty products used by women to keep men from reading between the lines. Unknown

A glamour girl is the girl who has less sense than others but seems to make more sense to men. Unknown

Females are not the only species who prostitute themselves for money; they are the only ones that are honest about it. Frank Dane

Quotes on Sex, Love & Marriage

No self-made man ever did such a good job that some woman didn't want to make a few alterations. Kin Hubbard

Faithful women are all alike, they think only of their fidelity, never of their husbands. Jean Giraudoux

My notion of a wife at forty is that a man should be able to change her, like a bank note, for two twenties. Douglas Jerrold

A gold digger is the woman who never lets money make a fool out of her, but always makes money out of a fool. Unknown

A gossip is a breeze stirred up by a couple of windbags. Unknown

A newspaper is a portable screen behind which a man hides from the woman who is standing up in a bus. Unknown

A modern novel is a story in which men are portrayed and women betrayed. Unknown

Middle age is the time of your life when a night out is followed by a day in. Unknown

Radiation is an X-ray that can reveal a lot about a man, though not as much as his ex-wife can. Unknown

A procrastinator is a person who has the right aim in life but never pulls the trigger. Unknown

Quotes on Sex, Love & Marriage

Being prompt is arriving at a date in time to wait. Unknown

A private secretary is a female assistant who knows more than the boss's wife, but tells less. Unknown

Sure men were born to lie, and women to believe them. John Gay

There are two times when you can never tell what is going to happen. One is when a man takes his first drink; and the other is when a woman takes her latest. O. Henry

A man who won't lie to woman has very little consideration for her feelings. Olin Miller

He's the sort of fool who thinks a woman loves him just because he loves her. W. Somerset Maugham

Men are nervous of remarkable women. James M. Barrie

A private secretary is the only person who knows more about the boss's affairs than the switchboard operator. Unknown

A psychiatrist is a woman's best friend because he spends so much of his time listening to her. Unknown

A pushover is a girl who in fishing for a man doesn't know where to draw the line. Unknown

Quotes on Sex, Love & Marriage

Putter is a woman's word for the work her husband does when he busies himself around the house. Unknown

Middle age is the time when you are still young, but only once in a while. Unknown

Intuition is the feminine sense that makes a woman's guess more accurate than a man's certainty. Unknown

The hospital is an institution where both husbands and wives get breakfast in bed. Unknown

The fickleness of the women I love is only equaled by the constancy of the women who love me. George Bernard Shaw

A woman must never let a man get accustomed to her absence. Lucas Cleeve

No man has ever yet discovered the way to give friendly advice to any woman, not even to his own wife. Honore De Balzac

When you hit seventy, you eat better, you sleep sounder, you feel more alive than when you were thirty. Obviously, it's healthier to have women on your mind than on your knees. Maurice Chevalier

Middle age is when a man doesn't look as young as he feels , or the woman who doesn't feel as young as she looks. Unknown

Quotes on Sex, Love & Marriage

A practical nurse is one who marries a wealthy patient.
Unknown

Perfume is a fragrant liquid used by women because men are easily led by the nose. Unknown

A necktie is a man's article of dress that his wife can always match better to his clothes. Unknown

A movie star is a beautiful bubble that's constantly being blown up by a press agent. Unknown

You know what a woman's curiosity is? Almost as great as a man's! Oscar Wilde

Debate is masculine; conversation is feminine. Bronson Alcott

The rooster makes more racket than the hen that lays the egg. Joel Chandler Harris

Illness offers a man a double advantage. To escape from himself and get the better of his wife. T.S. Eliot

A multimillionaire is the only man whose wife finds it hard to live beyond her husband's income. Unknown

A nurse is a young woman who holds your hand and strokes your forehead and expects your temperature to go down.
Unknown

Quotes on Sex, Love & Marriage

Overexposure is a term in television for the man who shows himself too much, or the woman who shows too much of herself. Unknown

Pregnancy is a condition that begins with a maternity dress and is sometimes followed by a paternity suit. Unknown

A middle-age spread is when the torso become more so. Unknown

A nurse is a hospital attendant who checks the patients' pulses, but more often their impulses. Unknown

An office is a place of business where the first thing a new girl learns is which men are still single. Unknown

A secret is a confidence women can keep just as well as men, but it takes more of them to do it. Unknown

Sarcasm is the art of saying what you want to say and getting out of range before it is understood. Unknown

A revolving door is a device that tends to make both men and women pushy. Unknown

"Why isn't your wife riding the burro?" asked the indignant white man of the mountain Indian whose wife trudged behind, her head buried beneath a huge bundle of household goods. "Ain't her burro," was the sensible reply. John Greenway

Quotes on Sex, Love & Marriage

Married women show all their modesty the first day, because married men show all their love the first day. William Wycherley

Don't make yourself a mouse or the cat will eat you. A.B. Cheales

Men are seldom right when they guess at a woman's mind. Sir George Etherege

As soon as women belong to us, we no longer belong to them. Michel De Montaigne

Scandal is letting the cat out of the bag, one claw at a time. Unknown

In the battle of the sexes, a man who hesitates is lost, but the woman who hesitates is won. Unknown

At any age the ladies are delightful, delectable and, most important, deductible. Goodman Ace

Women like silent men. They think they are listening. Marcel Achard

A man in trouble must be possessed, somehow, of a woman. Henry James

Quotes on Sex, Love & Marriage

Women hate revolutions and revolutionists. they like men who are docile, and well regarded at the bank, and never late at meals. H.L. Mencken

A cigarette is a man's refuge when he cannot face a woman's eyes. R. Halifax

In Genesis it says that it is not good for a man to be alone, but sometimes it is a great relief. John Barrymore

Men like to win; but women hate to lose. The difference can be summed up in one word: bridgemanship. Charles Goren

Behind every man with pull is a woman with push. Dean Robert H. Felix

The woman who is known only through a man is known wrong. Henry Adams

You see dear, it is not true that woman was made from man's rib; she was really made from his funny bone. James M. Barrie

What appears to be intuition in a woman-is often only transparency in a man. Jim Bishop

A woman's guess is much more accurate than a man's certainty. Rudyard Kipling

All a man could say of any woman was, what next? Edwin Lanham

Quotes on Sex, Love & Marriage

I'm not a woman hater. Life is only long enough to allow even an energetic man to hate one woman-adequately. Frank Richardson

He is a fool who thinks by force or skill to turn the current of a woman's will. Samuel Turke

Chivalry is the courtesy and respect of a man for a strange woman. Unknown

A bachelor is the man who has mental reservations about turning a sentimental girl into a temperamental wife. Unknown

An amateur is the young man who is afraid of overdoing it when flattering a woman. Unknown

A considerate motorist is one who will give a woman half of the road if he knows which half she wants. Unknown

Women will be as pleasing to men as whiskey when they learn to improve as much with age. Unknown

With women cooking is a weapon to catch men by the stomach and then watch it grow with the years. Unknown

We do not desire a thing because we adjudge it to be good, but, on the contrary, we call it good because we desire it. Spinoza

Quotes on Sex, Love & Marriage

Chutzpah is the audacity that enables a man sitting in a bus to flirt with a woman who is standing. Unknown

What difference does it make whether the women rule, or the rulers are ruled by women? The result is the same. Aristotle

The man who says his wife can't take a joke forgets that she took him. Unknown

A bachelor girl is one who often makes a hit with men but never makes a home run. Unknown

Chivalry is the consideration a man has for any woman who is pretty and isn't married to him. Unknown

A compliment is something that pleases a woman more than flowers and costs a lot less. Unknown

A compliment is proof that there's nothing like a little flattery to make a woman respect your judgment. Unknown

A coed is a college girl who didn't get her man in high school. Unknown

A confirmed bachelor is a womanizer with enough confidence in his judgment of women to act upon it. Unknown

Conscience is the inner voice that warns you to have an alibi. Unknown

Quotes on Sex, Love & Marriage

A coed is a college girl who, the more forward she is with men, the more backward she is in her studies. Unknown

Coeducation is a system under which a girl learns at college to separate the men from the boys. Unknown

Quotes on Sex, Love & Marriage

Quotes on Family and Everything Else

The golden wedding anniversary is a celebration of an enduring marriage where only the married couple knows how much each of them has endured. Unknown

A family quarrel is a fiery argument between a man and wife, often due to an old flame. Unknown

Encouragement is giving a person a shot in the arm without letting him feel the needle. Unknown

Help people reach their full potential. Catch them doing something right. Fortune Cookie Wisdom

A divorce lawyer is a marriage canceler. Unknown

We are not made of iron or steel. We are just human and need support, love and care. Isa Torrão

Cunning is a woman's method of getting around her husband by hugging him. Unknown

Courteous is being well-mannered enough to say and do the right thing at the right time in the right way. Unknown

Death and love are the two wings that bear the good man to heaven. Michael Angelo

Quotes on Sex, Love & Marriage

O, what a tangled web we weave, when first we practice to deceive. Walter Scott

Husbands are awkward things to deal with; even keeping them in hot water will not make then tender. Mary Buckley

Of all the joys that brighten suffering earth, what joy is welcomed like a new-born child? Caroline Norton

There comes a moment in our lives when we feel alone, we feel scared as we can't solve some problems by ourselves. And this is the moment when we wish a person, a person who keeps us safe and will be there for us. Unknown

Credit is the means to live beyond one's means. Unknown

God could not be everywhere, and therefore he made mothers. Jewish Proverb

A do-it-yourselfer is a man who can quickly turn a dripping faucet into a flowing stream. Unknown

Failure is not defeat until you stop trying. Fortune Cookie Wisdom

Entertainment is any pleasant pastime that makes time pass. Unknown

Quotes on Sex, Love & Marriage

The family is the household where the big responsibilities are the little ones. Unknown

A quarrel is an angry disagreement during which there is nothing less appreciated than clever sarcasm. Unknown

A gossip is one who loves to discuss the events of the day, neighbor by neighbor. Unknown

Home is the place where woman works in the absence of man, and man rests in the presence of woman. Unknown

When in doubt, just take the next small step. Fortune Cookie Wisdom

A garage sale is the conversion of trash into cash. Unknown

Divorce is a settlement where the husband does not always get the better of the better half. Unknown

The family is a group of related people that will stay together if they play together. Unknown

Children today are tyrants. They contradict their parents, gobble their food, and tyrannize their teachers. Socrates

When you see a married couple coming down the street, the one who is two or three steps ahead is the one that's mad. Helen Rowland

Quotes on Sex, Love & Marriage

The only time a woman wishes she were a year older is when she is expecting a baby. Mary Marsh

A man can't get rich if he takes proper care of his family. Navajo Proverb

Everybody is overworked. Now the main occupation of the educated man is not his job, but helping his wife at home. Margaret Mead

Money will buy a pretty good dog, but it won't buy the wag of his tail. Josh Billings

Just wait for the right moment. Keep your eyes and ears peeled. Fortune Cookie Wisdom

Only those who get into scrapes with their eyes open can find the safe way out. Logan Smith

Among a husband's other uses, most wives find him a handy thing with which to impress other women. Charles Morton

The family is a household where the parents do lots of talking and the children do little listening. Unknown

Divorce is a legal split-up where you cast off one mate and end up with someone else's castoff. Unknown

Quotes on Sex, Love & Marriage

A garage sale is the method of distributing the junk in one garage among the other garages in the neighborhood.
Unknown

Home is the place where some wives realize they talk to themselves, while others think their husbands are listening.
Unknown

A homebody is the woman who marries for a home, and then becomes married to it. Unknown

The husband staggered home at 4 A.M. and was met at the door by his outraged wife. "What excuse have you for getting here at this outrageous hour?" she demanded. Right away he answered, "Breakfast!" Unknown

A credit plan allows you to live within your income and beyond your means at the same time. Unknown

Compatibility is the ability of the wife to adjust her ideas of interior decoration to her husband's ideas of comfort.
Unknown

Make sure to laugh everyday...it's good for your health.
Fortune Cookie Wisdom

Our dreams were just wisps of heat above the morning coffee, gone as our love turned tepid, then cold. Robert H. Williams

Quotes on Sex, Love & Marriage

Having a little inflation is like being a little pregnant, inflation feeds on itself and quickly passes the "little" mark. Dian Cohen

Money never goes to jail. Arab Proverb

It's as hard to get a man to stay home after you've married him as it was to get him to go home before you married him. Helen Rowland

You grow up the day you have your first real laugh at yourself. Ethel Barrymore

A man never wakes up his second baby just to see it smile. Grace Williams

There is no pleasure in having nothing to do; the fun is in having lots to do and not doing it. Marry Little

A faithful wife becomes the truest and tenderest friend, the balm of comfort, and the source of joy; through every various turn of life the same. Savage

A wife is essential to great longevity; she is the receptacle of half a man's cares, and two-thirds of his ill-humor. Chas. Reade

A marriage is compatible where he makes the living and she makes living worthwhile. Unknown

Quotes on Sex, Love & Marriage

A computer is a mathematical machine that can figure out all kinds of problems, except the things in this world that just don't add up. Unknown

Cunning is a man's ability to convince his wife that a woman looks stout in a fur coat. Unknown

A dandelion is another thing which, if given an inch will take a yard. Unknown

Debt is the first thing a man runs into when he buys a car. Unknown

Husband calling his wife to the phone: "Darling someone wants to listen to you." Unknown

He who is shipwrecked the second time cannot lay the blame on Neptune. Fortune Cookie Wisdom

Triumphant father to mother watching their sixteen-year-old son mow the lawn: "I told him I lost the car keys in the tall grass." Unknown

How to keep your teenage daughter out of hot water: put some dishes in it. Unknown

It was a wise and experienced mother who announced to a gaggle of young fry at her son's birthday party, "Now remember kids, there will be a special prize for the little boy who goes home first." Unknown

Quotes on Sex, Love & Marriage

A trigger-tempered boss caught an employee reading the newspaper during working hours and barked: "When you get to the Help Wanted ads, start making notes." Unknown

On a Las Vegas divorce lawyer's door: "Satisfaction guaranteed, or your honey back." Unknown

Focus on trusting your intuition and you will get through it. Fortune Cookie Wisdom

Leisure time is when your wife can't find you. Unknown

There ought to be a better way to start the day than by getting up in the morning. Unknown

Any man whose actions leave his wife speechless has hit on a gold mine. Unknown

The test of a happily married - and wise woman is whether she can say, "I love you" far oftener than she asks, "Do you love me". Dorothy Dayton

One of the many things nobody ever tells you about middle age is that it's such a nice change from being young. Dorothy Canfield Fisher

The harder you fall, the higher you bounce. American Proverb

Quotes on Sex, Love & Marriage

I think somehow, we learn who we really are and then live with that decision. Eleanor Roosevelt

God, for two people to be able to live together for the rest of their lives is almost unnatural. Jane Fonda

A movie on TV is just like a wife, it's home and it's free. Unknown

The only book that really tells you where to go on your vacation is your check book. Unknown

I finally discovered the perfect way to get rid of dishpan hands, I let my husband do the dishes. Unknown

Second wives always work out better. Like it says in the ads, when you're number two, you try harder. Unknown

If you want to write something that will live forever, sign a mortgage. Unknown

Christmas is the time of year to get the kids something for the old man to play with. Unknown

Christmas is when you buy this year's gifts with next year's money. Unknown

A novice bowling wife to a would-be helpful spouse: "If I do anything wrong and you can show me how to do it better, keep your big mouth shut!" Unknown

Quotes on Sex, Love & Marriage

The Supreme Court of the United States gave a man the right to open his wife's letters, but it doesn't give him the courage. Farmer's Almanac

The people who get up early in the morning must have uncomfortable beds or disagreeable bedfellows. Unknown

Shortest bedtime story: "Move over!" Unknown

My wife found a new way to save her money, she uses mine. Unknown

One of the most wonderful gifts to send a mother-in-law on Mother's Day is her daughter. Unknown

An optimist is a guy who expects his wife to help him with the dishes. Unknown

There are two kinds of party-goers, one who wants to stay late and one who wants to leave early. The only trouble is, they are usually married to each other. Unknown

A man can always tell what kind of time he has been having at a party by the look on his wife's face. Unknown

Going to a party with your wife is like going fishing with the game warden. Unknown

Quotes on Sex, Love & Marriage

One thing about children, they never go around showing snapshots of their grandparents. Unknown

Nothing will improve your driving like having a police car following you. Unknown

Most of us spend a lifetime going to bed when we're not sleepy and getting up when we are. Unknown

One embarrassing thing about science is that it is gradually filling our homes with appliances smarter than we are. Unknown

A husband is a man who would do less lying if his wife didn't ask so many questions. Unknown

Happiness is the inner joy that can be sought or caught, but never taught or bought. Unknown

The cost of living is the amount you earn plus 20 percent. Unknown

A clotheshorse is a woman who wears herself out shopping for clothes, while her husband wears himself out paying for them. Unknown

Character is something formed in youth and reformed in marriage. Unknown

Quotes on Sex, Love & Marriage

The better half is the wife, so called because she usually gets the better of the other half. Unknown

A boy is a child whose idea of peace on earth is to beat a drum and blow a horn. Unknown

A woman has two smiles that an angel might envy; the smile that accepts a lover before words are uttered, and the smile that lights on the first-born babe, and assures it of a mother's love. Haliburton

Desert remains for a moment or two in your mouth and for the rest of your life on your hips. Peggy Bracken

Brilliant daughter, cranky wife. Dutch Proverb

The only real stumbling block is fear of failure. In cooking you've got to have a what-the-hell attitude. Julia Child

To be trusted is a greater compliment than to be loved. J. Macdonald

It is in those acts which we call trivialities that the seeds of joy are forever wasted. George Eliot

A boy is a youngster who loves his dog because it's the only thing around the house that doesn't find fault with him. Unknown

Quotes on Sex, Love & Marriage

A child is a stomach entirely surrounded by curiosity.
Unknown

A cocktail party is a party where they cut sandwiches and friends into little pieces. Unknown

The cost of living is the reason why a man pays more and more for a haircut as he has less and less hair to cut. Unknown

Credit is the financial trick that enables us to spend what we haven't got. Unknown

Happiness is something we'd never be able to appreciate if it weren't for our troubles. Unknown

A husband is a married man who sometimes bosses the house, but more often merely houses the boss. Unknown

A teenager is a girl who can do her homework in less time than it takes her mother to do the dishes. Unknown

A traffic light is where the speedy and the slow meet.
Unknown

A traveling salesman is one who should leave his wife long enough to increase her appreciation, but not long enough for her to seek consolation. Unknown

A widow is a woman who seldom appreciates her first husband until after she marries her second. Unknown

Quotes on Sex, Love & Marriage

A wife is the continual buzzing in a man's ear. Unknown

Happiness is when you invite your in-laws to dinner and they can't make it. Unknown

Oh, how bitter a thing it is to look into happiness through another man's eyes! Shakespeare

Cleaning your house while your kids are still growing is like shoveling the walk before it stops snowing. Phyllis Diller

Nobody's family can hang out the sign "Nothing the matter here." Chinese Proverb

No man is responsible for his father. That is entirely his mother's affair. Margaret Turnbull

Men are generally more careful of the breed of their horses and dogs than of their children. Penn

Inflation is when you earn four dollars an hour and in the supermarket your wife spends at the rate of six dollars a minute. Unknown

A wife is the most expensive answering service. Unknown

A triangle is what makes or breaks a marriage, depending on whether the third member is a baby or another woman. Unknown

Quotes on Sex, Love & Marriage

Triplets are twins with a spare. Unknown

A teenager is a girl whose parents have stopped trying to bring her up and have started trying to keep up with her. Unknown

Divorce court is the institution that has done the most to promote peace in the world. Unknown

A credit card is a device invented because money can't buy everything. Unknown

Alimony is giving comfort to the enemy. Unknown

An allowance is another thing a child outgrows rapidly. Unknown

A baby is a little cherub whose wings grow shorter as his legs grow longer. Unknown

Wife to husband: "You say I'm overdrawn - I say you're underdeposited." Unknown

The future destiny of the child is always the work of the mother. Napoleon

Drinking is something to do while getting drunk. Peggy Bracken

Quotes on Sex, Love & Marriage

Before fathers and mothers, uncles and aunts, itch as you may, you dare not scratch. Chinese Proverb

Never go to bed mad, stay up and fight. Phyllis Diller

What I know about money, I learned the hard way, by having had it. Margaret Halsey

Most people spend their lives going to bed when they're not sleepy and getting up when they are. Cindy Adams

All that I am, or hope to be, I owe to my angel mother. Lincoln

But one thing on earth is better than the wife, and that is the mother. L. Schafer

Wife: I wish to God that you wouldn't keep rubbing your great greasy belly against the back of my chair. Unknown

A baby is the only person who is admired for opening his mouth and putting his foot in it. Unknown

A baby-sitter is a teenager who behaves like a grown-up while the grown-ups are out behaving like teenagers. Unknown

A credit card is a convenient device that saves you the trouble of counting your change. Unknown

A critic is one who finds a little bad in the best of things. Unknown

Quotes on Sex, Love & Marriage

Divorce court's purpose is to put a lot of marriageable men back in circulation. Unknown

A do-it-yourselfer is the man who fixes everything himself, and then wonders why nothing in his house works. Unknown

Adolescence is the age when a teenager discovers that hard work takes all the fun out of earning money. Unknown

An alarm clock is the most common device used to awaken men, except their wives' elbows. Unknown

A bargain hunter is a woman whose husband is always surprised at the great diversity of things she would rather have than money. Unknown

The bathroom is the only room in some homes where you can have a few minutes to yourself. Unknown

A boy is a small creature who brings into a home a lot of happiness - also a lot of dirt, noise and junk. Unknown

A husband is a man who gives his wife the best ears of his life. Unknown

Music washes away from the soul the dust of every-day life. Auerbach

Quotes on Sex, Love & Marriage

Do you know how helpless you feel if you have a full cup of coffee in your hand and you start to sneeze? Jean Kerr

A father is a banker provided by nature. French Proverb

Always behave as if nothing had happened no matter what has happened. Arnold Bennett

Good manners are made up of petty sacrifices. Emerson

Where there is room in the heart there is always room in the house. Moore

A good laugh is sunshine in a house. Thackeray

A husband is a person who lays down the law to his wife and then accepts all her amendments. Unknown

A boy is a youngster who would love to go to the moon for his country, but hates to go to the supermarket for his mother. Unknown

A brat is the wild child who should end up end up. Unknown

Breakfast is the meal during which a husband reads while his wife is talking, or a wife talks while her husband reads. Unknown

A bridge player is a man who gets a real kick out of the game, but only when he sits opposite his wife. Unknown

Quotes on Sex, Love & Marriage

Character is something you either have or are. Unknown

A child is a youngster who alternates between being a lump in the throat and a pain in the neck. Unknown

Childhood is the time of life when we love to spend hours in a pool, but hate to spend minutes in a bathtub. Unknown

Child training is teaching a child good manners at his mother's knee - and across his father's. Unknown

Divorce court changes a situation from united we stand to divided we can stand it better. Unknown

A do-it-yourselfer is the man who stands out in a crowd like a sore thumb, with a sore thumb. Unknown

A domestic quarrel is a disagreement that often turns the better half into the bitter half. Unknown

Divorce is the proof that marriage is often a mirage. Unknown

Conscience is the guilty feeling resulting from cold feet. Unknown

Adolescence is the time of life when boys and girls start wondering what to do about their parents. Unknown

Quotes on Sex, Love & Marriage

Christmas is the season when a woman never knows what to give her husband until she learns how much he wants to spend for it. Unknown

The wife who drives from the back seat isn't any worse than the husband who cooks from the dining room table. Unknown

Alimony is the high cost of leaving. Unknown

A dining room table with children's eager, hungry faces around it, ceases to be a mere dining room table, and becomes an altar. Simeon Strunsky

Laughter is heard farther than weeping. Jewish Proverb

How sharper than a serpent's tooth it is to have a thankless child. Shakespeare

It's in your moments of decision that your destiny is shaped. Fortune Cookie Wisdom

Failure is the only opportunity to begin more intelligently. Fortune Cookie Wisdom

Alimony is the cash surrender value of the American male. Unknown

Explore your own world by working together with your friends. Fortune Cookie Wisdom

Quotes on Sex, Love & Marriage

It is not how much we have, but how much we enjoy, that makes happiness.   Spurgeon

If she go not as you would have her, cut her off from your flesh, and give her a bill of divorce and let her go. The Bible

Nagging is the constant repetition of an unpleasant truth. Unknown

Alimony is matrimonial insurance for women paid for by men for having poor judgement. Unknown

A wife is the person who sits up with you when you are sick, and puts up with you when you are not. Unknown

Wife to husband: " I was just as unreasonable when we were first married, but you thought it was cute." Unknown

A Christmas gift is one that a husband usually receives a month before he gets the bill. Unknown

Conscience is that part of human personality that is soluble in alcohol. Unknown

Divorce is the key that unfastens the lock of wedlock. Unknown

The father is the parent who is sometimes the master in his own home, but more often merely the paymaster. Unknown

Quotes on Sex, Love & Marriage

The earth is three quarters covered by water, and the other quarter covered by mortgages. Unknown

An economizer is a married man with a large family. Unknown

Economy is what a woman thinks she is practicing when she doesn't spend anything on her husband's needs. Unknown

Divorce is the pardon from the life sentence of matrimony. Unknown

A cosigner is a fool with a pen. Unknown

Credit is the clever way of permitting everyone to owe money to everyone else. Unknown

Without hearts there is no home. Byron

Perfect trust requires no pledges. Indian Proverb

The first indication of domestic happiness is the love of one's home. Montlosier

The small courtesies sweeten life; the greater, ennoble it. Bovee

Credit is something that's much easier to get for what you buy than for what you do. Unknown

Quotes on Sex, Love & Marriage

A dandelion is a weed that flowers like a sun and then blooms like a moon. Unknown

A dinner is a meal that parents sit down to eat while their children sit down to continue eating. Unknown

Discipline is training your children so that they get everything that's coming to them, whether it's good or bad. Unknown

Discretion is the wisdom of closing your eyes to a situation before someone else closes them for you. Unknown

Dish washing is a chore that can be avoided only when you have your husband eating out of your hand. Unknown

Divorce is the refuge for those who do not favor a fight to the finish. Unknown

Economy is what every married woman is ready to practice if her husband is willing to give her the money to practice it. Unknown

The family is a group of people kept together by small children, especially when they can't hire a baby-sitter. Unknown

The father is the parent who always talks about the good old days, but tells his children how much better they have it nowadays. Unknown

Quotes on Sex, Love & Marriage

The father-in-law is the only man who often supports two wives without being a bigamist. Unknown

The family album is the best argument for the styles of the present day. Unknown

The family budget is the plan of a family to live beyond its yearnings. Unknown

A domestic quarrel is a head-on collision where she loses her head and he blows his top. Unknown

The dishwasher is a husband who is also a part-time wife. Unknown

Divorce is a legal device designed to separate a married couple before the police do. Unknown

A clotheshorse is the wife who is easy to look at but hard to look after. Unknown

Domestic happiness is the end of almost all our pursuits, and the common reward of all our pain. Fielding

If you want peace in the house, do what your wife wants. African Proverb

No money is better spent that what is laid out for domestic satisfaction. Johnson

Quotes on Sex, Love & Marriage

A clotheshorse is the woman who finds it easier to hang on to her husband than to his money. Unknown

A cocktail party is a social gathering where alcohol removes the polish from both the furniture and the guests. Unknown

Divorce is what happens when the spouse who once seemed appealing now seems appalling. Unknown

A domestic quarrel is a dispute where both husband and wife say what they think without thinking. Unknown

A family budget is a spending plan made up of a little money and a lot of estimates. Unknown

The family budget is a method of thrifty expenditure that consists mostly in worrying about what became of last month's money. Unknown

A family man is one whose wallet is filled with more snapshots of his family than credit cards. Unknown

A family quarrel is a heated argument where everyone talks and no one listens - except the neighbors. Unknown

A domestic quarrel is an argument between husband and wife in which she lies about him and he tells the truth about her. Unknown

Quotes on Sex, Love & Marriage

The father is the head of the family, which is why he's the one who gets the headaches. Unknown

Incompatible is the marriage of the man who is a failure in making money to the woman who is a success in spending it. Unknown

Housework is a form of work that's like threading beads on a string with no knot on the end. Unknown

Happiness is something that sneaks in through a door you don't know you left open. Unknown

The golden wedding anniversary is a joyous one because by that time the happy couple is usually out of debt. Unknown

The saddest thing that can befall a soul is when it loses faith with God and woman. Alexander Smith

If you ever need a helping hand, you'll find one at the end of your arm. Yiddish Proverb

A castle after all is but a house-the dullest one when lacking company. James Sheridan Knowles

A graduate is a person who can no longer find the answers to his problems in the back of the textbook. Unknown

A grandfather is a grandchild's press agent. Unknown

Quotes on Sex, Love & Marriage

A grandmother is an inherited baby-sitter. Unknown

Happiness is keeping on good terms with everyone and everything, especially your conscience, your wife, and your stomach. Unknown

An heirloom is a possession handed down to an adult who wasn't allowed to handle it as a child. Unknown

A helpmate is the woman who helps her husband make money, or the man who helps his wife spend it. Unknown

A henpecked husband is the husband who is spouse-broken. Unknown

If you have a job without aggravations, you don't have a job. Fortune Cookie Wisdom

A husband is something no respectable wife should be without. Unknown

Housework is a form of unpleasant work to which a husband gives the best years of his wife. Unknown

Incompatible is the marriage of a man who has more income than he needs, to a woman who needs more income than he has. Unknown

A husband is a man who can do anything his wife puts her mind to. Unknown

Quotes on Sex, Love & Marriage

Homework is one of the few things a child is punished not for doing, but for not doing. Unknown

When the children all play in, the parents are usually played out. Unknown

A family is a group of kindred where the child's word is a wish, the father's word is an order, and the mother's word is law. Unknown

Divorce is a fifty-fifty settlement of the property, where one gets the house and the other gets the mortgage. Unknown

It is not by the gray of the hair that one knows the age of the heart. Bulwer

A glutton is one who digs his grave with his teeth. French Proverb

A divorce' is the man who stops bringing money home to his wife and starts mailing it. Unknown

A domestic quarrel is an argument that begins with what is right, and soon descends to who is right. Unknown

The family is a social unit where the father is concerned with parking space, the children with outer space, and the mother with closet space. Unknown

Quotes on Sex, Love & Marriage

The family album is an old book showing the evils of snap judgment. Unknown

The father is the parent who finds it impossible to practice half the things he preaches to his son. Unknown

Homework is a task given to schoolchildren to show them how much their parents don't know. Unknown

A household is the place that small children mark up with more fingerprints than are kept by the FBI. Unknown

A husband is a man who has lost his liberty in pursuit of happiness. Unknown

Marriage is the change from living within your income to living within your credit. Unknown

An infant is the only creature that's more helpless than its new-born father. Unknown

I can remember when the air was clean and sex was dirty. George Burns

A husband is the only man who is destined never to see his wife a widow. Unknown

A household is a house full of antique furniture if the family has money, or a house full of old furniture if the family has kids. Unknown

Quotes on Sex, Love & Marriage

A housekeeper is a woman who, every time she gets divorced, keeps the house. Unknown

A wife is expected by the husband to keep up appearances and keep down expenses. Unknown

A housewife is a married woman whose spouse is seldom a househusband. Unknown

Home is where you can scratch anyplace that itches. Unknown

Happiness is having enough money to live on, but not enough to worry about. Unknown

A henpecked husband is the most popular type of domestic help. Unknown

The dew of compassion is a tear. Byron

The greatest love is a mother's; then comes a dog's; then comes a sweethearts'. Polish Proverb

I can never close my lips where I have opened my heart. Dickens

A henpecked husband is the man who consults his better half instead of his judgment. Unknown

Quotes on Sex, Love & Marriage

Home is the place where we are treated the best, and yet grumble the most. Unknown

A housewife is one who reaches for a chair when answering the telephone. Unknown

A husband is the most important labor-saving device ever invented for women. Unknown

An infant is a small creature who soon ceases to be an armful and grows into quite a handful. Unknown

Infant care is something usually learned from the bottom up. Unknown

In a gentle way, you can shake the world. Fortune Cookie Wisdom

Insomnia is an ailment that babies commonly pass on to their parents. Unknown

Marriage is an equal partnership where he makes the money and she makes the decisions. Unknown

Marriage is an institution where a woman changes her ways, and a man his woes. Unknown

Parenthood is an art whose first step consists in snatching some sleep when the baby isn't looking. Unknown

Quotes on Sex, Love & Marriage

Monogamy is a union in which no man can serve two masters, unless he has a wife and grown-up daughter. Unknown

Marriage is a legal union where he rules the roost, and she rules the rooster. Unknown

A husband is the only thing which, if kept constantly in hot water, will not grow tender. Unknown

A housewife is a woman who, when it comes to housework, likes to do nothing better. Unknown

A grandmother is a baby-sitter who doesn't raid the refrigerator. Unknown

A family is a group of people where one generation grows vertically while the other generation grows horizontally. Unknown

One of the most common disrupters of marital bliss is the choice of where to spend a vacation. What this country needs is an ocean in the mountains. Paul Sweeney

If you tell people to live together, you tell them to quarrel. African Proverb

Diogenes was asked what wine he like best; and he answered as I would have done when he said: "Somebody else's." Montaigne

Quotes on Sex, Love & Marriage

The family is a social unit where the father does the providing, the mother the deciding, and the children the overriding. Unknown

Father's Day is a holiday similar to Mother's Day, except that you buy a much cheaper gift. Unknown

The florist is the only man who profits by the husbands who have lost arguments with their wives. Unknown

The difficulties of life are intended to make us better, not bitter. Fortune Cookie Wisdom

A fool's paradise is the marriage where the wife is the boss but the husband doesn't know it. Unknown

A fur coat is an outer garment that fattens the figure and slims the wallet. Unknown

A grandmother is an elderly lady that keeps you from spanking your child. Unknown

A housewife is a home appliance that works better not when new, but after years of service. Unknown

A husband is a man who has to wait impatiently for hours for his wife to be ready in a few minutes. Unknown

Marriage is a partnership that a man forms, and his mother-in-law reforms. Unknown

Quotes on Sex, Love & Marriage

A monologue is the conversation between a man and his wife.
Unknown

A mortgage is the thing about a home that gets the most interest. Unknown

A mother hopes for her son to be what she once thought her husband was. Unknown

Parenthood is the period when you discover your own ignorance by trying to answer your child's questions. Unknown

A mother-in-law is one whose shortcoming is her long staying. Unknown

A married man is a man who wishes he were as smart as he thinks his wife thinks he is. Unknown

Marriage turns a lover who is different into a husband who is indifferent. Unknown

The ideal wife is a woman who makes her hubby her hobby. Unknown

A husband is a married man who always knows at least one woman who has a wonderful mate. Unknown

A housewife is a woman who wonders why newspapers don't print more recipes and less sports news. Unknown

Quotes on Sex, Love & Marriage

Happiness is getting something you want but didn't expect. Unknown

Conscience is the still, small voice that you wish you could teach not to interrupt you. Unknown

Divorce is an outlet for the dissolution of marriage following the disillusion with love. Unknown

A cocktail party is where the cocktails consist of one part whiskey and two parts gossip. Unknown

Do not take life too seriously. You will never get out of it alive. Elbert Hubbard

You need a strong stomach to digest good luck. Russian Proverb

A domestic quarrel is a sharp clash during which you always remember to bring up things you ought to forget. Unknown

Happiness is the way station between too much and too little. Unknown

A housewife finds her daily toil most tedious not because it's housework, but because it's so daily. Unknown

House work is the only job where the work is steady but the pay isn't. Unknown

Quotes on Sex, Love & Marriage

A husband is a man you never really get to know if you meet him only when his wife is around. Unknown

The ideal wife is the woman who thinks she has an ideal husband. Unknown

Marriage is an occupation in which the toughest task for many a woman is to make a man out of a man. Unknown

A married man is a person who doesn't understand that his wife does understand him. Unknown

Marriage is what men and women do with each other when they don't know what to do with themselves. Unknown

Matrimony is the only business where the bosses are more often women than men. Unknown

A mother-in-law is an outspoken relative who is seldom outspoken. Unknown

A mother is a highly imaginative female who really believes that her children are as smart as she tells people they are. Unknown

Marriage is an institution where one and one not only make two but three or four or more. Unknown

Quotes on Sex, Love & Marriage

Incompatible is the marriage between a man to whom saving is a habit, and a woman to whom extravagance is an art. Unknown

A husband is a man who does not live by bread alone but needs buttering up from time to time. Unknown

Home is a convenient place to get out of wet socks and into a dry martini. Unknown

A henpecked husband is a domestic animal trained to wash up and dry up, but never act up. Unknown

No job is so simple that it cannot be done wrong. Fortune Cookie Wisdom

Happiness is the inner contentment of being married to your best friend. Unknown

A domestic quarrel is an angry dispute between husband and wife in which nothing is ever said that hasn't already been thought. Unknown

Success is like dealing with your kid or teaching your wife to drive. Sooner or later you'll end up in the police station. Fred Allen

The naked man never mislays his wallet. Japanese Proverb

Quotes on Sex, Love & Marriage

Nothing makes a man and wife feel closer, these days, than a joint tax return. Gil Stern

A domestic fight is an argument in which a smart husband knows just the right thing to say, but a smarter husband doesn't say it. Unknown

Happiness is filling a child's stomach, a woman's wardrobe, and a man's wallet. Unknown

A henpecked husband is the married man who was first hooked, then booked, and finally cooked. Unknown

Home is where the place where the husband runs the show but the wife writes the script. Unknown

A husband is the only man who has learned that there are some things you can't say with flowers. Unknown

Incompatibility is the friction between a boring husband who is always talking and a chattering wife who is never listening. Unknown

Marriage is an institution where half the husbands do not half appreciate their better halves. Unknown

A mother is one who never realizes the full value of education until summer is over and the children go back to school. Unknown

Quotes on Sex, Love & Marriage

Retirement is the time when you never do all the things you intended to do when you would have the time. Unknown

A spouse is a man who is either the master of the home or the paymaster. Unknown

Suburbia is a way of life whose disadvantage is that your neighbors are always buying something you can't afford. Unknown

Success is the difference between doing good and making good. Unknown

Summer is the season when parents pack up their troubles and send them to camp. Unknown

A teenager is a girl to whom a parent's experience is not the best teacher but the worst preacher. Unknown

A toy is something designed for use by children but for sale to adults. Unknown

Vacation is recreation where you take along twice as much clothing as you need and only half as much money. Unknown

A wife is a female whose privilege it is to change her mind, but whose practice it is to change her husband's. Unknown

Quotes on Sex, Love & Marriage

A vacation is a rest of two weeks that are too short, and after which you are too tired to return to work, and too poor not to.
Unknown

A wife is a contradictory creature who complains she hasn't a thing to wear, and then spends hours deciding what to put on.
Unknown

A toy is a plaything bought for a child whose first reaction is to find out how it breaks. Unknown

A teenage girl's arms are always too tired to do the dishes but her legs are never too tired to dance. Unknown

Summer is the season when children slam the same doors they used to leave open all last winter. Unknown

Success is the art of buying your experience cheap and selling it at a profit. Unknown

A suburbanite is one who finds mowing his lawn hard work, especially when he tries to make his son do it. Unknown

A spouse is the only relative who contests his wife's will while she's alive. Unknown

Retirement is the period in the life of a married couple when the wife has twice as much husband on half as much income.
Unknown

Quotes on Sex, Love & Marriage

There are two occasions when a man's past life is brought up before him, when he is drowning, and when he quarrels with his wife. Unknown

Rush hour is the traffic jam when there are long lines of cars everywhere going nowhere on their way to somewhere. Unknown

Poetic justice is the marriage of the man who knows it all to the woman who tells it all. Unknown

Mother's Day is a holiday celebrated by letting mother cook a bigger dinner than on any other Sunday. Unknown

A woman would make a better wife if she were not so busy making a better husband. Unknown

A nag is the wife who never runs out of conversation because she knows all about her husband's past. Unknown

A mother does not want her daughter to do the things she did as a child. Unknown

Marriage is a business in which the husband is the silent partner. Unknown

An infant is the only male a women ever succeeds in changing. Unknown

Quotes on Sex, Love & Marriage

A husband is a convenient object around the house to blame things on. Unknown

A hobo is the character to whom we owe a debt of gratitude for pioneering the cookout. Unknown

Home is the place where mother knows best - until the daughter takes a course in home economics. Unknown

Nothing makes you more tolerant of a neighbor's noisy party than being there. Franklin P. Jones

There are always two sides to a prediction. Gypsy Proverb

First you forget names, then you forget faces, then you forget to pull your zipper up, then you forget to pull your zipper down. Leo Rosenberg

The household is a battleground where the children always triumph unless both parents unite to defend themselves. Unknown

A home is where a mother spends half her time doing things, and the other half keeping the children from undoing them. Unknown

A housewife is the woman who not only reads her husband like a book, but gives the neighbors reviews. Unknown

Quotes on Sex, Love & Marriage

Housework is the work you do that no one notices unless you don't do it.   Unknown

A husband is a male animal that is sometimes caught, but more often trapped. Unknown

An infant is proof that there is nothing so powerful as a powerless baby. Unknown

Marriage is a universal custom where habit is often mistaken for fidelity. Unknown

A mother is the person who first arranges a match for her daughter, and then tries to referee it. Unknown

A nag is a woman who, knowing that the way to a man's heart is through his stomach, is always jumping down his throat. Unknown

Poetic justice is the irony when an egotist who is always talking about himself, marries a gossip who is always talking about other people. Unknown

A police woman's husband often takes the law into his own hands. Unknown

Popularity is the art of always paying attention, debts, and compliments. Unknown

A problem child is one who no's his own father. Unknown

Quotes on Sex, Love & Marriage

Parenting is a skill made much more difficult by having children of your own. Unknown

Go to the elders when you feel a confidence crisis. Fortune Cookie Wisdom

Parents are people who bore teenagers and board newlyweds. Unknown

Nostalgia is yearning for first childhood days while waiting for second childhood. Unknown

A mother is the person who remains sane only because she never knows what her three-year-old is going to do next. Unknown

Maturity is the mental ability to influence a teenager, convince a man, and persuade a woman. Unknown

Marriage is the only state that allows a woman to work eighteen hours a day. Unknown

A juvenile delinquent is the youngster who prefers vice to advice. Unknown

Indigestion is the incompatibility between the stomach of a man and the cooking of his wife. Unknown

Quotes on Sex, Love & Marriage

A husband is a man who, even when he has a model wife, cannot help looking over the later models. Unknown

I have discovered the secret formula for a carefree old age: ICR=FI, "If you Can't Recall it, Forget It." Goodman Ace

It's a wise man who lives with money in the bank, its a fool who dies that way. French Proverb

We are all here for a spell, get all the good laughs you can. Will Rogers

A man-of-the-hour is the one whose wife told him to wait a minute. Dr. Laurence Peter

Money is gratifying, not satisfying. Fortune Cookie Wisdom

A husband is a male who, after seeing the kind of men most women marry, realizes how lucky his wife is. Unknown

Indigestion is the stomach discomfort you get not only for what you eat, but for some of the things you have to swallow. Unknown

A juvenile delinquent is the youngster who has been given a free hand, but not in the proper place. Unknown

Marriage is where a wife will differ from a husband, but a husband always differs with her. Unknown

Quotes on Sex, Love & Marriage

Maturity is what enables a father to know almost as much as his adolescent son thinks he knows. Unknown

A mother is a parent who is embarrassed when her child tells lies, and even more embarrassed when he tells the truth. Unknown

Nostalgia is longing back to the good old days when we were neither good nor old. Unknown

Parents are people who wonder why their neighbor's children are so destructive while their own are merely mischievous. Unknown

Parents are people who spend half their time wondering how their children will turn out, and the rest of the time when they'll turn in. Unknown

A parking space is one that usually disappears while you are making a U-turn. Unknown

A problem child is a minor who is his parent's major problem. Unknown

A mother-in-law is a woman who thinks the bridegroom is not good enough for her own daughter, but too good for another woman's daughter. Unknown

A neighbor is one who seems to know more about your affairs than you do. Unknown

Quotes on Sex, Love & Marriage

A mother-in-law is the only law under which you are presumed guilty until proven innocent. Unknown

A mother is a parent who, just about the time she thinks her work is done, becomes a grandmother. Unknown

Matrimony is a partnership where a man earns money five days a week, while his wife spends money seven days a week. Unknown

Marriage is a partnership where no matter how good a husband is, his wife is still the better half. Unknown

A husband is a married man who knows there's no place like home, especially visiting in-laws. Unknown

Heredity is the traits that a disobedient child gets from the other parent. Dr. Laurence Peter

Inflation is a condition of economic instability that turns a nest egg into chicken feed. Unknown

Hatred is like fire; it makes even light rubbish deadly. George Eliot

A husband is a man whose duty it is to keep talking to unexpected guests at the front door while his wife straightens out the living room. Unknown

Quotes on Sex, Love & Marriage

An ideal husband is the husband every married woman thinks some other woman has. Unknown

Marriage is a 5O-5O proposition because 5O couples stay married for every 5O couples that get divorced. Unknown

The middle class try to live in public as the rich do, by living in private as the poor do. Unknown

A miracle drug is the medicine a child will take without a struggle. Unknown

A mother is not worried by what her daughter knows but how she found it out. Unknown

A mother-in-law is a woman who always knew her son would never get as good a wife as his father got. Unknown

A neighbor is a woman who will spend half an hour talking at a door because she hasn't time to come in. Unknown

Being neighborly is talking to your neighbors instead of about them. Unknown

A nervous breakdown is a collapse caused by spending half your time keeping your mind on your work, and the other half keeping your work on your mind. Unknown

A nest egg is an egg that's feathered with cash down. Unknown

Quotes on Sex, Love & Marriage

New Year's Eve is a holiday when the old year ends with the people mixing drinks, and the new year begins with the drinks mixing people. Unknown

Optimism is expecting your wife to drive a car 6 feet wide through a garage doorway 8 feet narrow. Unknown

The outdoors is something brought into a home by picture windows, or more often by a couple of small children. Unknown

Overindulgence is the pursuit of happiness that leads to unhappiness. Unknown

A parent is the common enemy that drives grandparents and grandchildren together in mutual affection. Unknown

Parenthood is a gradual process that turns a bright son of fourteen into a foolish father at forty. Unknown

A mother-in-law is the matrimonial kin that gets under your skin. Unknown

A monogamist is a man who is contented with one wife - usually his own. Unknown

Mother is the person who sits up with you when you are sick, and puts up with you when you are well. Unknown

Quotes on Sex, Love & Marriage

Money is the fringe benefit of the job you enjoy. Unknown

Marriage is a relationship in which no woman gets everything she expects, and no man expects everything he gets. Unknown

A husband is what every woman should have to share her joys and sorrows - and her friends' secrets. Unknown

Middle age is a time of life that a man first notices in his wife.
Richard Armour

Take care of your pennies and your dollars will take care of your widow's next husband. American Proverb

A husband is a man who seldom acknowledges his faults, so as not to deprive his wife the pleasure of pointing them out.
Unknown

Marriage is a form of gambling because a woman never knows in advance how much her alimony will be. Unknown

Money is the only thing that keeps your credit card in good standing. Unknown

A mother is the parent to whom the only thing necessary to make children bright is for them to be her own. Unknown

A mother-in-law is a woman who often goes too far while remaining too near. Unknown

Quotes on Sex, Love & Marriage

Parenthood is a gamble because you never know hor far you're going to be driven out of your mind. Unknown

Parenthood is the only job that requires no experience to achieve but considerable experience to perform. Unknown

Old age is when we prefer siestas to fiestas. Unknown

A mother is a parent whose endurance is never really put to the test until the television set breaks down during a rainy weekend. Unknown

Marriage is a matter of stress and strain: the wife always stresses her need for more things, while the husband strains to provide them. Unknown

A husband is a man who finds it easier to live with two hundred pounds of curves than a hundred pounds of nerves. Unknown

The ideal husband is the man who thinks his wife's arthritis is as important as his own headache. Unknown

In each human heart are a tiger, a pig, an ass and a nightingale. Diversity of character is due to their unequal activity. Ambrose Bierce

Never do card tricks for the boys you play poker with. American Proverb

Quotes on Sex, Love & Marriage

The ideal husband is one who is smart enough to earn a lot of money, and foolish enough to give it all to his wife. Unknown

Marriage is a plan where a man is the thermometer and a woman the temperature, with the thermometer always subject to changes of temperature. Unknown

Married life is the period when you make progress when you break even. Unknown

A mother worries that some scheming female will ensnare her son, and that no scheming male will ensnare her daughter. Unknown

Motherhood is the relief a woman experiences after all the children are in bed. Unknown

A mother-in-law is a referee with a vested interest in one of the combatants. Unknown

Old age is the time of life when the little grey-haired lady you help across the street is your own wife. Unknown

An old flame will often set off an explosion in the home. Unknown

Parenthood is the period when having to set a good example for your children takes all the fun out of life. Unknown

Quotes on Sex, Love & Marriage

A parking space is something you see when you haven't got your car. Unknown

Perfume is the gift a man buys his wife if he loves her but doesn't like the way she smells. Unknown

Parents are permissive when they don't mind if their children don't mind. Unknown

A suburb is a residential section where an obnoxious family always has better neighbors than they have. Unknown

To be upset over what you don't have is to waste what you do have. Fortune Cookie Wisdom

A skinflint is the man who lets his wife spend money like water, drip, drip, drip. Unknown

Slander is hearing something you like about somebody you don't. Unknown

A slap is a blow often used to make a foolish youngster smart. Unknown

Sleep is the only thing that can keep a boy quiet and out of mischief at the same time. Unknown

Sleeptalking is what some men resort to when they want their wives to listen to what they say. Unknown

Quotes on Sex, Love & Marriage

Small fry are little people who tear up the house but seldom break up a home. Unknown

Children are the only people wise enough to enjoy today without regretting yesterday or fearing tomorrow. Unknown

A small town is a place where everyone knows whose credit is good and whose wife isn't. Unknown

A smile is the universal language that even a baby understands. Unknown

A soap opera is a serial drama in which it takes 11 months to have a premature baby. Unknown

Soft soap is what you apply when you get a dirty look from your wife. Unknown

A spa is a health resort for recycling one's fat. Unknown

Spanking is a form of punishment inflicted on one end to impress the other. Unknown

A shopping cart is one of the most expensive vehicles to drive. Unknown

A shrew is a wife whose strength lies in her husband's weakness. Unknown

Quotes on Sex, Love & Marriage

Imagination is something that will always sit up with a woman when her husband comes home very late. Unknown

A husband can wait all day for his dinner, but not five minutes more. Unknown

Incompatible is the marriage between a man of few words and the woman of a few million. Unknown

It's far easier to forgive an enemy after you've gotten even with him. Olin Miller

Papa's having and Mama's having is not like having one's self. Chinese Proverb

A man who can be a hero to his wife's relations may face the rest of the world fearlessly. Meredith Nicholson

A shrew is another woman who lives a double life, hers and her husband's. Unknown

Spanking is a punishment that takes less time than reasoning and penetrates sooner to the seat of the memory. Unknown

A split-level is the type of home whose ownership is split between the resident and the mortgage company. Unknown

A split-up is a marital separation usually leading to a divorce suit because nothing but a divorce seems to suit. Unknown

Quotes on Sex, Love & Marriage

A spouse is a lover whose face is unshaved, pants unpressed, and stomach out of order. Unknown

A suburb is a residential district laid out by first cutting down the trees and then naming the streets after them. Unknown

Success is what a man never really achieves until his mother-in-law admits it. Unknown

Pleasure is an agreeable feeling caused by getting the last laugh, having the last word, or paying the last installment. Unknown

A popular song is a melody that makes us all believe that we can really sing. Unknown

Power is the ability to control others, sometimes by pushing people down, sometimes by pulling them up. Unknown

The only thing sweeter than receiving praise is the feeling of having deserved it. Unknown

A predicament is an awkward situation in which a wife cries and a husband lies. Unknown

Pregnancy is the shape of things to come. Unknown

Prenatal is the only period in a person's life when his name cannot be found on a mailing list. Unknown

Quotes on Sex, Love & Marriage

Presence of mind is the ability, when you are up to your neck in trouble, to use the part that isn't submerged. Unknown

A preteen is a child too old to need a baby-sitter and too young to act as one. Unknown

A resort is a place where people spend money they haven't earned, to buy things they don't need, to impress people they don't like. Unknown

Respect is the belief that the girl you marry is better than the girls you go out with. Unknown

A retiree is the husband who is usually a wife's full-time job. Unknown

Marriage is a union in which some women will follow a man to hell, while others prefer to send him there alone. Unknown

Realism is hoping for the best, expecting the worst, and accepting whatever comes. Unknown

A realist is the father who doesn't give his son all the allowance he can afford but keeps some back to bail him out. Unknown

Puberty is the age when a boy starts walking around a puddle instead of through it. Unknown

A problem child is the youngster who has been spoiled by getting everything, except punishment. Unknown

Quotes on Sex, Love & Marriage

A mother is the parent who no sooner stops sitting up with her children than she starts sitting up for them. Unknown

Marriage is a school of experience where some men learn rapidly, while others still argue with their wives. Unknown

There are lots of good women who, when they get to heaven, will watch to see if the Lord goes out nights. Ed Howe

A grain of luck is better than an ass's load of destiny. Persian Proverb

Grandchildren don't make a man feel old; it's the knowledge that he's married to a grandmother. G. Norman Collie

Marriage is a union where the husband's dues for the rights of membership amount to his whole take-home pay. Unknown

A nightgown is a napsack. Unknown

A nursery school is where small children go to catch colds from one another so they can stay home. Unknown

A problem child is an irresponsible youngster who is responsible for a lot of trouble. Unknown

Puberty is the period when children stop asking questions and begin to question answers. Unknown

Quotes on Sex, Love & Marriage

A realist is one who realizes the highest price you can pay for anything is to get it for nothing. Unknown

A refrigerator is a place used to store leftovers until they are ready to be thrown out. Unknown

Remarriage is a legal device that increases the divorce rate because divorced couples refuse to stay divorced. Unknown

Remote control is the name for a man's control of his wife. Unknown

Marriage is a committee of two on ways and means, with the woman getting her way and the man supplying the means. Unknown

A retiree is a man who stops lying about his age and starts lying about the house. Unknown

Retirement is a state of leisure that takes all the pleasure out of weekends. Unknown

Marriage is a process that gradually turns a chivalrous knight into an appetite that needs a shave. Unknown

Loyalty is sticking with your husband through all the trouble he wouldn't have had if he hadn't married you. Unknown

Lucky is the forgetful man whose wife found the letter he forgot to mail but not the one he forgot to burn. Unknown

Quotes on Sex, Love & Marriage

Man spends part of his time before marriage trying to get ahead, but most of his time after marriage trying to get along. Unknown

Marriage is the state of wedded bliss where husband and wife usually think alike, with the wife always having the first think. Unknown

A nag is a woman who robs her husband of his peace of mind by constantly giving him a piece of hers. Unknown

Repartee is a clever retort made by you that becomes even cleverer when you tell about it afterward. Unknown

Retirement is the time in life when there is nothing so difficult as doing nothing. Unknown

Puberty is the period when a youngster begins to eat again even before the dishes have been washed. Unknown

Marriage is an institution where every man is free to choose his own form of government - blonde, brunette, or redhead. Unknown

The husband who doesn't tell his wife everything probably reasons that what she doesn't know won't hurt him. Leo J. Burke

Wisdom is born, stupidity is learned. Russian Proverb

Quotes on Sex, Love & Marriage

There is only one thing for a man to do who is married to a woman who enjoys spending money, and that is to enjoy earning it. Ed Howe

Marriage is an institution in which the woman who chooses her husband's clothes, probably started out by choosing his wife. Unknown

A married man is the kind of man that makes the best husband. Unknown

Puberty is the period when youth accepts being ruled by parents, but objects to being overruled by them. Unknown

Retirement is the period whose chief drawback is that you limited to only one social security number. Unknown

Rush hour is the time of day when a motorist travels the shortest distance in the longest time. Unknown

A schoolteacher is an adult who handles many more children than a parent, and is given two months' vacation every year to recuperate. Unknown

A nag sends her husband to an early grave with a series of little digs. Unknown

Marriage is another union whose members always have trouble with management. Unknown

Quotes on Sex, Love & Marriage

Long - suffering is the husband whose wife remembers everything. Unknown

Leisure is the spare time a housewife has in which to do some other kind of work. Unknown

The life of the party is the husband who acts older than he is at home, and younger than he is at parties. Unknown

Marriage is a highly overrated institution where many a husband can be easily be replaced by a heating pad. Unknown

The value of marriage is not that adults produce children but that children produce adults. Peter De Vries

The best times of your life have not yet been lived. Fortune Cookie Wisdom

It is useless to go to bed to save the light, if the result is twins. Chinese Proverb

A married man with a family will do anything for money. Charles Talleyrand

I have certainly known more men destroyed by the desire to have a wife and child and to keep them in comfort than I have seen destroyed by drink and harlots. William Butler Yeats

Quotes on Sex, Love & Marriage

Marriage is an institution where you first get married and settle down, then you settle up and get divorced. Unknown

A mirage is a word that is close to marriage in spelling, and even closer in meaning. Unknown

A modern home is a place equipped with electronic appliances that can do anything you want done, except pay your electric bills. Unknown

A problem child was a rarity in the good old days when the problem was thrashed out in the woodshed. Unknown

Instant food is something that enables a housewife to prepare dinner in less time than it takes to get the family to the table. Unknown

Instinct is the natural tendency that makes a man turn to his wife when he's in trouble. Unknown

Puberty is the in-between age when a youngster is too old to say something cute and too young to say something sensible. Unknown

A quarrel is one of the few things left in married life that can still be made out of nothing. Unknown

A raise in the increase in pay you get just before going into a little more debt. Unknown

Quotes on Sex, Love & Marriage

Realism is taking things into consideration instead of taking them into court. Unknown

Remote control is a college student writing home for money. Unknown

A nag is a wife who may not know how to cook, but who certainly knows how to bring her husband to a boil. Unknown

A secret is something told in strict confidence, and repeated in strict confidence. Unknown

Self-assurance is being overweight, over fifty and wearing shorts while mowing the lawn. Unknown

Let there be magic in your smile and firmness in your handshake. Fortune Cookie Wisdom

Sense is what a wife has if she laughs at her husband's jokes even when they make no sense. Unknown

A sense of humor is a sense that is more common than common sense. Unknown

Marriage is a feminine plot to add to a man's responsibilities and subtract from his rights. Unknown

A wife is a woman who is willing to share everything with a man, but not her clothes closets. Unknown

Quotes on Sex, Love & Marriage

A traffic jam is the most uncomfortable distance between two points. Unknown

It you're riding ahead of the herd, look back once in awhile to make sure the it's still there. Fortune Cookie Wisdom

Success is something compounded of ambition, hard work, and marriage to the boss's daughter. Unknown

A teenager is the leading authority on adult education. Unknown

A supermarket is a large food store whose rising prices keep many a man out of the stock market. Unknown

Summer is the time of year when it's too hot to do the job that it was too cold to do last winter. Unknown

A suburb is a place where opportunity knocks but once and the neighbors the rest of the time. Unknown

A shrew is a woman who, when she wants her husband's opinion, gives it to him. Unknown

To bring up a child in the way he should go, travel that way yourself once in a while. Josh Billings

If parents would only realize how they bore their children. George Bernard Shaw

Quotes on Sex, Love & Marriage

A shrew is a married woman who can dish it out much better than she can cook it. Unknown

A suburb is a residential area connected to the city during rush hours by a long traffic jam. Unknown

Summer is the season when the dog days don't bother us as much as the mosquito nights. Unknown

A supermarket is the place where the number of cents a dollar is worth depends on the amount of sense the shopper has. Unknown

A tantrum is a fit of temper by a child's losing his head, usually followed by a mother losing hers. Unknown

Teenage is the period when adolescents feel their parents should be told the facts of life. Unknown

A traffic jam is a crowded line of cars where you sometimes drive five miles an hour and sometimes five hours a mile. Unknown

A wife is a woman whose idea of cooperation is to buy more clothes than her husband, but wear them less. Unknown

A shrew is a woman with a will of her own with her husband the sole beneficiary. Unknown

Quotes on Sex, Love & Marriage

Silence is something rarely found in men, women, or children. Unknown

A silent partner is the husband of a chatterbox. Unknown

A spouse is a married man who shouldn't be judged by the company he keeps, especially if they are his in-laws. Unknown

A teenager is an adolescent whose hang-ups do not include his clothes. Unknown

Twelve is the age when a preteen daughter starts to preen. Unknown

A wife is a woman who singles out a man, doubles his joys, and triples his expenses. Unknown

A vacation is the holiday that turns the worn-out into the played out. Unknown

A wife is a creature who, when her lips drip honey, is after some of her husband's money. Unknown

The vacation is the time off given to employees to remind them that the company can get along without them. Unknown

Whiskey is still the most useless remedy for a cold, and still the most popular. Unknown

Quotes on Sex, Love & Marriage

A teenager is an adolescent girl who seldom obeys anything but her impulses. Unknown

A spouse is a mate hard to take if he rarely comes home, and even harder to take if he hangs around the house all the time. Unknown

Spring is the silly season when men plant grass in order to slave in the summer keeping it cut. Unknown

A stalemate is a husband who keeps telling the same old jokes. Unknown

Statistics is numerical data that can prove women spend 85 percent of the consumer dollar, children 15 percent, and men the rest. Unknown

A shrew is a woman who never commands her husband's respect because she always makes him respect her commands. Unknown

The stomach is the only part of the body that ads fat instead of muscle when you exercise it. Unknown

The happiness of a married man depends on the people he has not married. Oscar Wilde

Nothing flatters a man as much as the happiness of his wife; he is always proud of himself as the source of it. Samuel Johnson

Quotes on Sex, Love & Marriage

The man who enters his wife's dressing room is either a philosopher or a fool. Honore de Balzac

One good thing about living on a farm is that you can fight with your wife without being heard. Kin Hubbard

A suburb is a place that has lost the joy of the country and lacks the fun of the city. Unknown

A thoughtful wife has the pork chops ready when her husband comes home from a fishing trip. Unknown

Thoughtfulness is holding the door open for your wife while she carries in a load of groceries. Unknown

A wife is the first and still the best type of lie detector. Unknown

Thrifty is the housewife who drives to the supermarket in a small, economy size car to buy large, economy size products. Unknown

A timesaver is a household appliance that enables a mother-in-law to spend more of her time interfering with her children. Unknown

A toddler is the morning caller, the noonday crawler, the midnight brawler. Unknown

Quotes on Sex, Love & Marriage

Tongued-tied is the man who can't break in because his wife can't break off. Unknown

A whisper is a trick parents resort to when they want their children to listen to what they are saying. Unknown

A wife is a creature easier to procure than to cure. Unknown

A martyr is a person who is married to a saint. Unknown

There's something much bigger than money, bills. Unknown

There are times when parenthood seems nothing but feeding the mouth that bites you. Peter de Vries

I shall be so polite to my wife as though she were a perfect stranger. Robert Jones Burdette

I don't have any trouble meeting my obligations. My trouble is ducking them. Unknown

Kids rarely misquote you, especially when they repeat what you shouldn't have said. Unknown

Most department stores are willing to give a woman credit for what her husband earns. Unknown

Today you need credit cards even if you want to pay cash. Unknown

Quotes on Sex, Love & Marriage

When I first met my wife she was always on a diet. She had an hourglass figure; but now she's let the sand settle in the wrong end. Unknown

The worst thing about a divorce is that somewhere, perhaps many miles apart, two mothers are nodding their heads and saying, "See, I told you so!" Unknown

Education is what a man get gets when he sits in his living room with a group of teenagers. Unknown

Executive ability is convincing your wife you hired your pretty secretary for her ability. Unknown

My eyes were never any good, and I've got a wife to prove it. Unknown

A wise man never laughs at his wife's old clothes. Unknown

If you want to drive your wife crazy, don't talk in your sleep, just grin. Unknown

My wife is a magician, nobody makes money disappear like her. Unknown

When one mother kept hollering, her daughter talked back: "Don't yell at me, I'm not your husband!" Unknown

Be kind to your mother-in-law, baby-sitters are expensive. Unknown

Quotes on Sex, Love & Marriage

Your getting old when you don't care where your wife goes, just so you don't have to go along. Unknown

Middle age is that time of life when you can feel bad in the morning without having had fun the night before. Unknown

Through greater effort and hard work a precious dream comes true. Fortune Cookie Wisdom

The best way to cure your wife of anything is to tell her it's caused by advancing age. Unknown

Alimony is something that enables a woman to profit by her mistakes. Unknown

Last week my wife and I celebrated our tin anniversary, ten years eating out of cans. Unknown

Every anniversary her husband takes a day off, and she takes a year off. Unknown

A wife is a woman who is seldom interested in what her husband is saying, unless he is talking to another woman. Unknown

When our children were small we thought they were brilliant. Now they're adolescents, and they think we're retarded. Unknown

Quotes on Sex, Love & Marriage

The three most important events of human life are equally devoid of reason: birth, marriage and death. Austin O'Malley

Humor is falling downstairs if you do it while in the act of warning your wife not to. Kenneth Bird

Youth is a time of rapid changes. Between the ages of twelve and seventeen a parent can age thirty years. Unknown

The simplest toy, one which even the youngest child can operate, is called a grandparent. Unknown

Any unmarried woman who has a baby and stays with it and raises it and loves it should be given the honorary degree of Mrs. Unknown

Wile is the trick of a wife who doesn't threaten to go home to mother, but threatens to invite mother for a month's visit. Unknown

A zipper is something that has done more than anything else to bring husbands and wives together. Unknown

Better to have loved your wife than never to have loved at all. Unknown

There is no change as sudden and disarming as the change in a woman's voice when she goes from bawling out her husband to answering the telephone. Unknown

Quotes on Sex, Love & Marriage

All I want is the right to sit at the steering wheel in the family car in front of the house at seven AM and honk the horn continuously for half an hour while my husband dresses the children for school. Unknown

Grant yourself a wish this year; only you can do it. Fortune Cookie Wisdom

Any husband who thinks he's smarter than his wife is married to a very smart woman. Unknown

Thank God I don't have to go to work. I just get out of bed in the morning and there it is, all around me. Unknown

A woman's place is in the home. Why should she go out and take away a working man's pay instead of staying home and stealing it out of his jacket like a good wife. Unknown

Woman wanted: to help in the house, 18-hour day, 7-day week, sleep in. Must have knowledge of cooking, sewing, medicine, law, child psychology, elementary electricity, bookkeeping and sex. Must be strong and willing. No wages, only room and board. Unknown

Minds are like parachutes. They only function when they are open. Fortune Cookie Wisdom

A recession is when your neighbor loses his job, a depression when the husband loses the job, and panic is when the wife loses her job. Unknown

Quotes on Sex, Love & Marriage

Give your husband enough rope and he will want to skip. Unknown

It now costs more to amuse a child than it did to educate his father. Unknown

A wife is a woman whose idea of thrift is to cut down on her husband's expenses. Unknown

I was a premature baby, my father wasn't expecting me. Unknown

The only thing worse than being a bachelor is being a bachelor's son. Unknown

My wife should run for Congress, nobody brings so many bills into the house. Unknown

Compatibility is the unconcern of a married couple about who is the better half. Unknown

Getting the right answer is only possible when you have asked the right question. Fortune Cookie Wisdom

A legal separation is a court decree under which a man and wife live together better when they are apart. Unknown

A wife is a frail craft sailing on the sea of matrimony, and the longer she sails, the craftier she becomes. Unknown

Quotes on Sex, Love & Marriage

The way to hold a husband is to keep him a little bit jealous. The way to lose him is to keep him a little bit more jealous. H.L. Mencken

Most wives are nicer than their husbands, but that's nothing. I am nice to everybody from whom I get money. Don Herold

A wife is a woman who has taken advantage of a man's marriage to her. Unknown

A sense of humor is the sense that never warns you what it is not safe to laugh at. Unknown

Comfort zones are most often expanded through discomfort. Fortune Cookie Wisdom

September is the month when the kids go back to school and their mothers go back to bed. Unknown

A shrew is the woman who thinks of a man before marriage and thinks for him afterward. Unknown

A wife is another disease that's easy to catch but hard to get rid of. Unknown

Incompatible is a marriage between a man who spends most of the time after money, and his wife who spends money most of the time. Unknown

Quotes on Sex, Love & Marriage

A henpecked husband is the type that never buys a suit on his own because he needs his wife to tell him whether he likes it or not. Unknown

Insomnia is a condition sometimes caused by an upset stomach but more often by an upset wife. Unknown

Intuition is the suspicion that enables a wife who knows less than her husband to understand more. Unknown

A joint account is a bank account where the husband is slow to put money in, but the wife is quick on the draw. Unknown

The kitchen is the place where woman's inhumanity to man makes countless cases of indigestion. Unknown

Las Vegas is a place where men shake dice and women shake their husbands. Unknown

A marriage is compatible when each spouse can see through the other and still enjoy the view. Unknown

A grouch is the only crossword puzzle that has no solution. Unknown

Housework is the only kind of work where a woman, when she has nothing to do, still has something to do. Unknown

A husband is what every woman should have, preferably her own. Unknown

Quotes on Sex, Love & Marriage

No matter how grouchy you're feeling,
You'll find the smile more or less healing.
   It grows in a wreath
   All around your teeth-
Thus preserving the face from congealing. Unknown

The ideal husband is surely not a man of active and daring mind; he is the man of placid and conforming mind. H.L. Mencken

A grouch escapes so many little annoyances that it almost pays to be one. Kin Hubbard

Any man who agrees with his wife can have his way.
Unknown

A husband is simply a lover with a two day's growth of beard, his collar off and a bad cold in the head. Unknown

A professor says that married men are much more inventive than single men. They have to be. Unknown

All husbands are alike but they have different faces so you can tell them apart. Unknown

To err is human; to remain in error is stupid. Unknown

The height of irony is to give father a billfold at Christmas.
Unknown

Quotes on Sex, Love & Marriage

Many a man who is a five-ton truck at the office is nothing but a trailer at home. Unknown

The best eraser in the world is a good night's sleep. Unknown

Summer camps: those places where little boys go for mother's vacation. Unknown

To be able to play with the kids and enjoy it, is a sure sign that you are still young. Unknown

The way to drive a baby buggy is to tickle its feet. Unknown

Nothing can cure a man of laziness; but a second wife will sometimes help. Unknown

That which you cannot give away, you don't possess; it possesses you. Fortune Cookie Wisdom

One often wonders where mothers learned all about the things they tell their daughters not to do. Unknown

Children are said to be delinquent when they get to the age where they want to do what their parents are doing. Unknown

You have to stay awake to make your dreams come true. Unknown

Quotes on Sex, Love & Marriage

The husband is the last to know the dishonor of his house. Unknown

A father is a man who can't get on the phone, into the bathroom or out of the house. Unknown

A yawn is the short period a married man gets to open his mouth. Unknown

A modern wife is a woman who knows what her husband's favorite dishes are and the restaurants that serve them. Unknown

Marriage is the only life sentence that can be suspended by bad behavior. Unknown

Where there's a will, there are relatives. Unknown

Blood is thicker than water - and it boils quicker. Unknown

Marriage is a period where you make progress if you break even. Unknown

Boy: a noise with some dirt on it. Unknown

Summer: the season when children slam the doors they left open all winter. Unknown

Alimony: bounty after the mutiny. Unknown

Quotes on Sex, Love & Marriage

There's no place like home after the other places close. Unknown

Intoxication: to feel sophisticated and not be able to pronounce it. Unknown

Desertion: a poor man's divorce. Unknown

The man who said 'talk is cheap' never had a wife with a charge account in a department store. Unknown

Why is there so much month left at the end of the money? Unknown

Many a man spanks his children for things his own father should have spanked out of him. Don Marquis

A man seldom thinks with more earnestness of anything that he does of his dinner. Samuel Johnson

A wife encourages her husband's egoism in order to exercise her own. Russell Green

A man never does justice to himself as an entertainer when his wife is around. Edgar W. Howe

Homemade dishes can drive one from home. Thomas Hood

A husband is one who, having dined, is charged with the care of the plate. Ambrose Bierce

Quotes on Sex, Love & Marriage

He who laughs last didn't get the point. Unknown

Who follows his wife in everything is an ignoramus. The Talmud

A successful man is one who can earn more than his wife can spend. Unknown

Marriage is a mutual partnership if both parties know when to be mute. Unknown

Alimony is the male's best proof that you have to pay for your mistakes. Unknown

A hangover is a condition you can avoid by staying drunk. Unknown

One must be perfectly stupid to be perfectly happy. Unknown

A wife is the person who can look in a bureau drawer and find her husband's cuff links that aren't there. Unknown

When the American husband gets as much appreciative fuss made over him for providing food, shelter, clothes, and education for the family as dogs get for bringing in the morning newspaper, there will be fewer divorces. Unknown

Discretion is when you are sure you are right, and then ask your wife. Unknown

Quotes on Sex, Love & Marriage

A luxury is anything a husband needs. Unknown

A wife is a woman who keeps breaking things, like five, ten, and twenty dollar bills. Unknown

Kids used to ask where they come from, now they tell you where to go. Unknown

A joint checking account is a handy little device that permits your wife to beat you to the draw. Unknown

A feast is made for laughter, and wine maketh merry, but money answereth all things. The Bible

Every man should eat and drink, and enjoy the good of all his labor. The Bible

An Irish alibi is the proof that you were in two places at the one time. Unknown

Murphy told Quinn that his wife is driving him to drink. Quinn thinks him lucky because his own wife makes him walk. Unknown

A cocktail party is a gathering where 10 percent of the guests eat 90 percent of the food. Unknown

Commencement is the day a college graduate commences to learn what life is really about. Unknown

Quotes on Sex, Love & Marriage

A commuter is a farmer with enough sense to work in the city or a city man with enough sense to live in the country. Unknown

The law is reason free from passion. Aristotle

Trust everybody, but cut the cards. Finley Peter Dunne

Conscience is what makes you tell your wife before someone else does. Kenneth Steier

There is more to life than increasing its speed. Mahatma Gandhi

It's nice for children to have pets - until the pets start having children. Dr. Laurence Peter

It is the parents' nature to clean up after their children; from the time they shit and piss their diapers to when they shit and piss in their lives. Robert Williams

Perhaps the saddest lot that can befall mortal man is to be the husband of a lady poet. George Jean Nathan

I have no trouble with my enemies. It is my damned friends, they' are the ones that keep me walking the floor nights. Warren G. Harding

I do desire we may be better strangers. William Shakespeare

Quotes on Sex, Love & Marriage

There are lots of people who can't think seriously without injuring their minds. John Chapman

Here lies my wife; here let her lie; now she's at rest and so am I. John Dryden

Middle age is when your age starts to show around your middle. Bob Hope

If advertising encourages people to live beyond their means, so does matrimony. Bruce Barton

The best inheritance a parent can give his children is a few minutes of his time each day. O.A. Battista

Babies: little rivets in the bonds of matrimony. Arthur Gordon

Be careless in your dress if you must, but keep a tidy soul. Mark Twain

Just think how happy you'd be if you lost everything you had right now, and then got it back again. Francis Rodman

Good will is the one and only asset that competition cannot undersell or destroy. Marshall Field

Great talkers are little doers. Benjamin Franklin

Quotes on Sex, Love & Marriage

The degree of one's emotions varies inversely with one's knowledge of the facts - the less you know the hotter you get.
Bertrand Russell

Laughter is a sudden sense of glory. Thomas Hobbes

Character is the result of two things - mental attitude and the way we spend our time. Elbert Hubbard

Character is made by what you stand for; reputation, by what you fall for. Robert Quillen

Every man who is high up loves to think that he has done it all himself; and the wife smiles, and lets it go at that. James M. Barrie

Experience achieves more with less energy and time. Oscar Wilde

Do what you can, with what you have, where you are.
Theodore Roosevelt

Never lose an opportunity of seeing anything beautiful. Beauty is God's handwriting. Charles Kingsley

An idealist is one who, upon observing that a rose smells better than a cabbage, concludes that it will also make better soup.
H.L. Mencken

Quotes on Sex, Love & Marriage

Divorce is a legal separation of two persons of the opposite sex who desire to respect and honor each other. Kin Hubbard

Being a husband is a whole-time job. That is why so many husbands fail. They cannot give their entire attention to it. Arnold Bennett

Act the way you'd like to be and soon you'll be the way you act. Dr. George W. Crane

Try praising your wife, even if it does frighten her first. Billy Sunday

Everyone is the hero of his own baptism, his own wedding, and his own funeral. Oliver Wendell Holmes

All happy families are alike, but every unhappy one is unhappy in its own way. Leo Tolstoy

Fun is like life insurance, the older you get, the more it costs. Kin Hubbard

It is necessary to be almost a genius to make a good husband. Honore de Balzac

When a husband and wife have got each other, the devil only knows which has got the other. Honore de Balzac

Friendships, like marriages, are dependant on avoiding the unforgivable. John MacDonald

Quotes on Sex, Love & Marriage

Married men are horribly tedious when they are good husbands, and abominably conceited when they are not. Oscar Wilde

One of the main conveniences of marriage is that if you can't stand a visitor you can pass him along to your wife. George Lictenberg

Happiness: a good bank account, a good cook, and a good digestion. Jean Rousseau

A hero is no braver than an ordinary man, but he is brave five minutes longer. Ralph Waldo Emerson

If the ends don't justify the means, what can? John Maynard Keynes

Being entirely honest with oneself is good exercise. Sigmund Freud

Human felicity is produced not so much by great pieces of good fortune that seldom happen, as by little advantages that occur every day. Benjamin Franklin

Divorce is a hash made of domestic scraps. Ed Wynn

You never realize how short a month is until you pay alimony. John Barrymore

Quotes on Sex, Love & Marriage

No blessing lasts forever. Plautus

My wife was too beautiful for words - but not for arguments. John Barrymore

Some people pay a compliment as if they expected a receipt. Kin Hubbard

The trouble with America is that there are far too many wide open spaces surrounded by teeth. Charles Luckman

Paper napkins never return from a laundry-nor love from a trip to the law courts. John Barrymore

You study one another for three weeks, you love each other for three months, you fight for three years, you tolerate the situation for thirty. Andre de Missan

Married life ain't so bad after you get so you can eat the things your wife likes. Frank Hubbard

A friend who cannot at a pinch remember a thing or two that never happened is as bad as one who does not know how to forget. Samuel Butler

A husband should tell his wife everything that he is sure she will find out. Thomas Dewar

The husband who desires to surprise is often very much surprised himself. Voltaire

Quotes on Sex, Love & Marriage

It destroys one's nerves to be amiable every day to the same human being. Benjamin Disraeli

A husband without faults is a dangerous observer. Sir George Savile

If you drink like a fish, don't drive, swim. Joe E. Lewis

Man does not live by words alone, despite the fact that sometimes he has to eat them. Adlai Stevenson

Of all the home remedies, a good wife is best. Kin Hubbard

There are moments when everything turns out right. Don't let it alarm you; they pass. Jules Renard

If you don't lose your mind over certain things, you haven't got a mind to lose. Johann Nestroy

You can't get rid of what is part of you, even if you throw it away. Goethe

Marriage without the spice of small quarrels is like a poem without rhyme. G.C. Lichtenberg

Let there be spaces in your togetherness. Kahil Gibran

There is a proverb, "As you have made your bed, so must you lie in it," which is simply a lie. If I have made my bed

Quotes on Sex, Love & Marriage

uncomfortable, please God, I will make it again. G.K. Chesterton

To forgive and forget is to throw valuable experience out the window. Arthur Schopenhauer

I believe in getting into hot water. I think it keeps you clean. G.K. Chesterton

A drunk sometimes cracks funnier jokes than the best of comedians. Vauvenargues

It is the hope and dreams we have that make us great. Fortune Cookie Wisdom

Clean your finger before you point at my spots. Benjamin Franklin

If you kiss enough asses you'll get kicked in the teeth. Gerald Barzan

We pay for the mistakes of our ancestors, and it seems only fair that they should leave us the money to pay with. Don Marquis

I don't have to look up my family tree, because I know that I'm the sap. Fred Allen

Every baby born in the world is finer than the last. Charles Dickens

Quotes on Sex, Love & Marriage

Beauty may be said to be God's trademark in creation. Henry Ward Beecher

Seeing is deceiving. It's eating that's believing. James Thurber

You can do anything with children if you only play with them. Otto Von Bismark

Children rule, old men go to school, women wear the breeches. Robert Burton

When children stand still, they have done some ill. A.B. Cheales

When children are doing nothing they are doing mischief. Henry Fielding

A mother loves her child more than the father does, because she knows it's her own, while the father only thinks it's his. Menander

Parents where invented to make children happy by giving them something to ignore. Ogden Nash

The thing that impresses me most about America is the way parents obey their children. Duke of Windsor

The things most people want to know are usually none of their business. Bernard Shaw

Quotes on Sex, Love & Marriage

The greater the fool the better the dancer. Theodore Edward Hook

Running into debt isn't so bad. It's running into creditors that hurts. Jacob M. Braude

Dreading the climax of all human ills, the inflammation of his weekly bills. Lord Byron

If you must choose between two evils, pick the one you've never tried before. Fortune Cookie Wisdom

You can fool too many of the people too much of the time. James Thurber

Th' first thing some folks put on after they git up in th' mornin' is a fresh grouch. Kin Hubbard

I sincerely regret all my divorces because I don't like anything to be unsuccessful. John Paul Getty

It is a great consolation for a man who has made a muddle of his life, to throw the blame on his wife, especially if he can get his wife to believe it. Frank Richardson

A woman, the more curious she is about her face is commonly the more careless about her house. Ben Johnson

Quotes on Sex, Love & Marriage

Where does the family start? It starts with a young man falling in love with a girl, no superior alternative has yet been found. Sir Winston Churchill

It is a melancholy truth that even great men have their poor relations. Charles Dickens

The child had every toy his father wanted. Robert C. Whitten

Yes, my fat goes under my belt, but yours goes under your hat. Finley Peter Dunne

A knowing wife, if she is worth her salt, can always prove her husband is at fault. Geoffrey Chaucer

It is curious that we should be more anxious to conceal our best passions than our worst. Walter Savage

Watch out that someone else's emotion does not grip your throat. Stanislaw J. Lec

Home is the girl's prison and the woman's workhouse. Bernard Shaw

Humor is your own smile surprising you in your mirror. Langston Hughes

Many married couples have learned that a joke can be the shortest distance between two points of view. J.P. McEvoy

Quotes on Sex, Love & Marriage

A husband should never let his wife visit her mother unattended. Honore De Balzac

Don't ever slam a door; you might want to go back. Fortune Cookie Wisdom

A husband should always know what is the matter with his wife, for she always knows what is not. Honore De Balzac

Life is short; live it up. Nikita Khrushchev

Man is the most intelligent of animals, and the most silly. Diogenes

Marriage is give and take. You'd better give it to her or she'll take it anyway. Joey Adams

Some husbands are born optimists. They go through life believing that somehow, somewhere, they eventually will arrive someplace on time, with their wife. It never happens. Hal Boyle

The Japanese have a word for it. It's judo - the art of conquering by yielding. The Western equivalent of judo is "Yes, dear." J.P. McEvoy

An empty head leads to an empty pocket. B.C. Forbes

Quotes on Sex, Love & Marriage

Here's to our town-a place where people spend money they haven't earned to buy things they don't need to impress people they don't like. Lewis C. Henry

It's a wise child that knows its own mother in a bathing suit. G.L. Apperson

My wife is the king of girl who'll not go anywhere with her mother, and her mother will go anywhere. John Barrymore

The mother's heart is the child's schoolroom. Henry Ward Beecher

If you keep your mouth shut you will never put your foot in it. Austin O'Malley

It's other folks' dogs and children that make most of the bad feelin's between neighbors. Ellis Parker Butler

A red nose is caused by sunshine or moonshine. Evan Esar

Your opinion of others is apt to be their opinion of you. B.C. Forbes

The rule of my life is to make business a pleasure and pleasure my business. Aaron Burr

Behold the turtle. He makes progress only when he sticks his neck out. James Bryant Conant

Quotes on Sex, Love & Marriage

More trouble is caused in the world by indiscreet answers than by indiscreet questions. Sydney J. Harris

A ship under sail, a man in complete armour, and a woman with a big belly, are three handsomest sights in the world. James Howell

Compliment three people every day. Fortune Cookie Wisdom

A cocktail party is a place where you talk with a person you do not know about a subject you have no interest in. Lin Yutang

The road to success is filled with women pushing their husbands along. Lord Thomas Robert Dewar

A man travels the world over in search of what he needs and returns home to find it. George Moore

A hole is nothing at all, but you can break your neck in it. Austin O'Malley

Some people want champagne and caviar when they should have beer and hot dogs. Dwight D. Eisenhower

However careful a man is, his wife always finds out his failings. James M. Barrie

The road to success is always under construction. Fortune Cookie Wisdom

Quotes on Sex, Love & Marriage

Commuter-one who spends his life
In riding to and from his wife;
A man who shaves and takes a train
And then rides back to shave again. E.B. White

There is no hope for men who do not boast that their wives bully them. G.K. Chesterton

A fair wife without a fortune is a fine house without furniture. Thomas Fuller

Fortitude is the guard and support of the other virtues. Fortune Cookie Wisdom

Don't build your happiness on other's sorrow. Fortune Cookie Wisdom

Some women seem t'be able t' entertain ever'buddy but their husbands. Kin Hubbard

Fear is interest paid on a debt you may not owe. Fortune Cookie Wisdom

Mistakes show us what we need to learn. Fortune Cookie Wisdom

I have learned that only two things are necessary to keep one's wife happy. First let her think she's having her way. And second, let her have it. Lyndon Johnson

Quotes on Sex, Love & Marriage

A modern wife is the prostitute who doesn't deliver the goods. W. Somerset Maugham

Man has found remedies against all poisonous creature, but none was yet found against a bad wife. Francois Rabelais

God save us all from wives who are angels in the street, saints in the church, and devils at home. Charles Haddon Spurgeon

The person who removes a mountain, can start the clean up too. Fortune Cookie Wisdom

Married women are kept women and they are beginning to find it out. Logan Pearsall Smith

Have faith in the force of right and not in the right of force. Fortune Cookie Wisdom

A meal without wine is a day without sunshine. Louis Vaudable

That a man of intellect has doubts about his mistress is conceivable, but about his wife!-that would be too stupid. Honore De Balzac

My wife's idea of housecleaning is to sweep the room at a glance. Joey Adams

Quotes on Sex, Love & Marriage

A wife is afraid of having her husband enjoy his work too much; she doesn't mind if he suffers at it-for her sake. Hal Boyle

If the grass is greener in the other fellow's yard, let him worry about mowing it. Fred Allen

Fear can keep us up all night long, but faith makes one fine pillow. Fortune Cookie Wisdom

Failure is the virtual way to prepare for great responsibilities. Fortune Cookie Wisdom

Only put off until tomorrow what you are willing to die having left undone. Fortune Cookie Wisdom

When science discovers the center of the universe a lot of people will be disappointed to find they are not it. Bernard Baily

Drinking makes such fools of people, and people are such fools to begin with, that it's compounding a felony. Robert Benchley

Most of today's families are broke. It will just take a depression to make it official. Gregory Nunn

Unquestionably, there is progress. The average American now pays twice as much in taxes as he formerly got in wages. H.L. Mencken

Quotes on Sex, Love & Marriage

Failure is the chance to do it better next time. Fortune Cookie Wisdom

Life moves on, whether we act as cowards or heroes. Fortune Cookie Wisdom

Money is not everything. You can buy a doctor but not your health. Fortune Cookie Wisdom

Imagination is more important than knowledge. Fortune Cookie Wisdom

Be kind to your mother-in-law; but pay for her board at some good hotel. Josh Billings

We secure our friends not by accepting favors but by doing them. Fortune Cookie Wisdom

A citizen of ancient Rome sought to divorce his wife, and as a result was severely chastened by his friends, who asked: "Was she not chaste? Was she not fair?" The Roman held out one of his shoes. "Is it not well made?" he said. "Is it not also new?" And when they agreed that the shoe was both well made and new, the Roman replied: "Yet none of you can tell where it pinches me." Plutarch

There is nothing more demoralizing than a small but adequate income. Edmund Wilson

Quotes on Sex, Love & Marriage

Look within. Within is the fountain of good, and it will ever bubble up, if thou wilt ever dig. Marcus Aurelius

If you don't enjoy what you have, how could you be happier with more? Fortune Cookie Wisdom

Why is it that, in spite of all the mirrors in the world, no one really knows what he looks like? Schopenhauer

What utter foolishness it is to be afraid that those who have a bad name can rob you of a good one. Seneca

The best thing in the world being a strong house held in serenity where man and wife agree. Homer

Once a child is born, it is no longer in our power not to love it nor care about it. Epictetus

Good books are friends who are always ready to talk to us. Fortune Cookie Wisdom

When a love-relationship is at its height, no room is left for any interest in the surrounding world; the pair of lovers are sufficient unto themselves, do not even need the child they have in common to make them happy. Freud

When disagreement rears its head,
My spouse and I don't fight:
We talk it over calmly 'til
We find out why she's right. Dick Emmons

Quotes on Sex, Love & Marriage

A bridge table is the only place I've seen where a wife is usually eager to do her husband's bidding. Charles Goren

Paying alimony is like having your TV set on after you've fallen asleep. Henny Youngman

Think for yourself or think for no-one. Fortune Cookie Wisdom

It is pleasant at times for a man to have a jealous wife; there is a constant mention of what he loves. LaRochefoucauld

How can we expect someone else to keep our secret if we cannot keep it ourselves. LaRochefoucauld

Just a dollop of liqueur for me to calm
Will undo the workings of my palm
Nor can I take a bowl of sweet herbal scent
For then my get up & go, just get up and went
So just give me the fracking Ciallis pills at $5 dollars a pop
And maybe, if I can calm myself, I'll be able to love myself to come-alot. Robert Williams

Reality must be truthful to be useful. Robert H Williams

If there's nothing to hide...why hide the information, objects or gag people or documents or loose emails violating Federal Law? Robert H Williams

Say what you mean and mean what you say. -unknown

Quotes on Sex, Love & Marriage

Don't make promises and policies you don't intend to keep and to keep the policies and promises you do make.   Robert H Williams

ACTIONS speak louder than words.
ACTIONS are PROOF of intent.
ACTIONS are the final judgment of character.
It REALLY is that simple. Robert H Williams

Who are you and what do you want?
When your heart is stopped and your breath is caught?
When you are between life and death are you aware?
Which places and choices you should beware?
What have you said? What did you mean?
Why are you here? Where have you been?
What have you done? What have you seen?
Where are you going? What will happen then?
Robert Williams

If you can't laugh at yourself, then you can't really laugh at all.
Robert H. Williams
===

Quotes on Sex, Love & Marriage

Quotes on Sex, Love & Marriage

www.ingramcontent.com/pod-product-compliance
Lightning Source LLC
Chambersburg PA
CBHW061630040426
42446CB00010B/1345